SCIENCE AND TECHNOLOGY IN JUDICIAL DECISION MAKING

CREATING OPPORTUNITIES AND MEETING CHALLENGES

MARCH 1993

A Report of the

CARNEGIE COMMISSION
ON SCIENCE, TECHNOLOGY, AND GOVERNMENT

ISBN 1-881054-08-X

Printed in the United States of America

CONTENTS

FOREWORD

This country was founded with a conviction that science and government are necessarily intertwined. The Founders' dedication to empiricism is exemplified in the Constitution's delegation to Congress of the power to advance science and technology through the issuing of patents. In the words of a modern scholar, "the importance of science was elevated for the first time in history to a position of authoritatively providing answers to questions of public policy."[1] Of late, this American faith in science has collided with what Alexis de Tocqueville termed our "legal habit," a certain litigiousness inherent in our commitment to individual rights and privileges. The result has been increasing friction between science and the law.

Since World War II, the government's involvement in science and technology has grown enormously. One aspect of this growth has been the creation of institutions to support both the executive and the legislative branches when they are called upon to make decisions on S&T matters. Even though our "legal habit" means that many of the most significant issues involving science emerge initially in our courts, the judiciary has received little external assistance and support.

From the outset, the Carnegie Commission on Science, Technology, and Government recognized that unique and important issues are raised by judicial decision making that involves scientific matters and that the judiciary receives too little interdisciplinary advice on how to respond to the challenges posed by the increasing intersection of science and the courts. For this reason, we consider the work of this task force to be among the most important undertakings of the Commission.

As Chief Justice Rehnquist's 1992 year-end report on the federal judiciary makes clear, isolation from different perspectives harms the judiciary and, in turn, all of us. At this historic moment, open communication and closer cooperation between branches is essential if the judiciary is to discharge its responsibilities effectively. In the case of S&T issues in the courts, such cooperative efforts must also reach out to members of the science and technology community.

We are pleased that the Task Force has been able to undertake a variety of initiatives to facilitate the interbranch and interdisciplinary dialogue that is necessary to ensure better judicial decision making on S&T issues. The Federal Judicial Center project described in this report marks a new era of cooperation, one that we believe will demonstrate the utility and viability of efforts to assist the judiciary in its adjudication of S&T matters.

Our country's faith in science and its commitment to judicial resolution of disputes ensure that the judiciary will continue to be called upon to decide questions on the frontiers of science; these questions will arise in cases that raise profound social, economic, and public policy concerns. The time has come to give the judiciary the support it needs to perform this difficult task.

We wish to thank the Task Force on Judicial and Regulatory Decision Making and particularly its chair, Helene Kaplan, for their outstanding work.

William T. Golden, Co-Chair
Joshua Lederberg, Co-Chair

PREFACE

This report of the Carnegie Commission on Science, Technology, and Government was prepared by its Task Force on Judicial and Regulatory Decision Making. The Commission was established in 1988 to assess the mechanisms by which each branch of government incorporates scientific and technological knowledge into its decisions and to propose improvements in process and organization. From its inception, the Commission recognized that the judiciary warranted special examination, and in early 1989 the Commission formed the Task Force to study this key aspect of governmental decision making. The Task Force appreciates the encouragement and support of its efforts by David A. Hamburg, President of Carnegie Corporation of New York, and of William T. Golden and Joshua Lederberg, co-chairs of the Commission.

The members of the Task Force were

<table>
<tr><td>Helene L. Kaplan, Chair</td><td>Joseph G. Perpich</td></tr>
<tr><td>Alvin L. Alm</td><td>Paul D. Rheingold</td></tr>
<tr><td>Richard E. Ayres</td><td>Maurice Rosenberg</td></tr>
<tr><td>Sheila L. Birnbaum</td><td>Oscar M. Ruebhausen</td></tr>
<tr><td>Stephen G. Breyer</td><td>Pamela Ann Rymer</td></tr>
<tr><td>Harry L. Carrico</td><td>Irving S. Shapiro</td></tr>
<tr><td>Theodore Cooper</td><td>William K. Slate, II</td></tr>
<tr><td>Douglas M. Costle</td><td>Patricia M. Wald</td></tr>
<tr><td>E. Donald Elliott</td><td>Jack B. Weinstein</td></tr>
<tr><td>Kenneth R. Feinberg</td><td></td></tr>
<tr><td>Robert W. Kastenmeier</td><td>Margaret A. Berger,
Senior Consultant</td></tr>
<tr><td>Donald Kennedy</td><td></td></tr>
<tr><td>Francis E. McGovern</td><td>Steven G. Gallagher,
Senior Staff Associate</td></tr>
<tr><td>Richard A. Merrill</td><td></td></tr>
<tr><td>Richard A. Meserve</td><td>David Z. Beckler,
Senior Advisor</td></tr>
<tr><td>Gilbert S. Omenn</td><td></td></tr>
</table>

The Task Force held its first meeting in November 1989, and numerous subgroup, committee, and task force meetings have taken place since then. Its first initiative in 1989 was to assist the Federal Courts Study Committee, which had just been established by Congress with members appointed by the Chief Justice of the United States, to survey the state of the federal judiciary. The Federal Courts Study Committee's final report in 1990 reflected several important issues raised by the Task Force. Acting on that report, the Judicial Conference of the United States acknowledged the increasing importance of economic, statistical, and natural and social scientific data in both routine and complex litigation and called upon the Federal Judicial Center to conduct a comprehensive examination of how courts handle complex scientific and technological issues.

Cooperative efforts, initiated by the Task Force with the Federal Judicial Center, culminated in a pilot project within the Federal Judicial Center to create a Science and Technology (S&T) Resource Center as an institutional base for examination of judicial management of S&T issues. The project will complete, disseminate, and maintain a S&T manual for federal judges; develop science and technology components for judicial education programs; identify needed research and planning to improve the judiciary's ability to handle S&T information; and engage the scientific and technical communities in these activities. The Task Force is deeply grateful to Judge William W. Schwarzer for his outstanding leadership of the Federal Judicial

Center, which has made it possible for this important initiative to become a reality.

The Task Force has also undertaken cooperative activities with the scientific community. These include an ongoing project with the Federal Judicial Center to prepare model protocols for judges that seek to disaggregate the complex issues surrounding scientific or technical evidence. In addition, the Task Force is providing assistance to other interdisciplinary efforts to examine and improve judicial decision making with regard to S&T issues: the ABA/AAAS National Conference of Lawyers and Scientists' examination of the issues surrounding court-appointed S&T experts; the Brookings Institution's plans to convene an Interbranch Symposium on Risk Management in 1993; and the RAND Institute for Civil Justice's preparation of a model of mass tort litigation.

In December 1992, the Commission filed an *amicus curiae* brief in a case before the Supreme Court of the United States. This brief, which builds on the work of the Task Force, concerns the standards for admissibility of S&T expert testimony. It proposes an integrated approach to scientific evidence that acknowledges and respects both the special expertise of science and the judge's responsibility to declare law. None of the judicial members of the Commission or the Task Force participated in any way in the decision to file a brief or in crafting the argument to present to the Court.

The brief and this final report were drafted principally by Margaret A. Berger, Senior Consultant to the Task Force. Her comprehensive knowledge of the issues and extensive practical experience have been of invaluable assistance to the Task Force throughout its deliberations. The Task Force also wishes to acknowledge with appreciation the editing of the manuscript by Jeannette L. Aspden and the fine contribution to this report of John Bender, Elizabeth H. Esty, Mark Schaefer, and others from within and outside the Commission. Finally, the Task Force expresses its gratitude to Commission staff members David Z. Beckler and Steven G. Gallagher, whose ideas, unfailing commitment, and energy were indispensable to the success of the Task Force.

This report was endorsed by the Task Force and adopted by the Commission at its meeting on November 30, 1992.

EXECUTIVE SUMMARY
BACKGROUND, FINDINGS, AND RECOMMENDATIONS

The courts' ability to handle complex science-rich cases has recently been called into question, with widespread allegations that the judicial system is increasingly unable to manage and adjudicate science and technology (S&T) issues. Critics have objected that judges cannot make appropriate decisions because they lack technical training, that jurors do not comprehend the complexity of the evidence they are supposed to analyze, and that the expert witnesses on whom the system relies are mercenaries whose biased testimony frequently produces erroneous and inconsistent determinations. If these claims go unanswered, or are not dealt with, confidence in the judiciary will be undermined as the public becomes convinced that the courts as now constituted are incapable of correctly resolving some of the most pressing legal issues of our day. There may be calls to replace the current system with new institutions and procedures that appear to be more suited to the demands of science and technology.

From the beginning of its work, therefore, the Task Force recognized the importance of obtaining as much information as possible about the handling of S&T issues by our courts. Its focus was primarily on the federal judiciary because of the advantages of studying and interacting with one system rather than fifty, and because many of the most pressing problems raised by science-rich cases are readily apparent in the federal courts, which have often been the forums of choice for toxic tort litigation involving such substances as Agent Orange, asbestos, the Dalkon Shield, and Bendectin. The Task Force has, however, also discussed these issues with state judicial systems through such organizations as the State Justice Institute and the National Center for State Courts.

We hope that the activities of the Task Force will counter the current uneasiness about judicial decision making with regard to scientific and technological issues. Our investigations have shown that, although there are problems with the handling of complex S&T issues, these difficulties are manageable within the present adversarial process. Indeed, many of the criticisms directed at the operation of our court system arise — quite understandably — from misperceptions about the differing methodologies and goals of science and law, and from the consequent failure to comprehend the diverse roles and expertise of "judge," "juror," and "scientist."

SCIENTIFIC "FACTS" AND THE JUDICIAL SYSTEM

Scientists view their work as a body of working assumptions, of contingent and sometimes competing claims. Even when core insights are validated over time, the details of these hypotheses are subject to revision and refinement as a result of open criticism within the scientific communities. Scientists regard this gradual evolution of their theories through empirical testing as the pathway to "truth." In the legal system, however, all of the players are forced to make decisions at a particular moment in time, while this scientific process is going on. Given the indeterminacy of science, how can the judicial system make the best use of a scientific "fact"? This question is at the core of the Task Force's efforts.

RECENT DEVELOPMENTS

Recent developments in both law and science have conspired to bring increasingly complex scientific issues before the courts for resolution. In particular, the dramatic growth in toxic torts and environmental litigation has put new pressure on the legal system, which is simultaneously being asked to adjudicate issues on the cutting edge of science and to develop theories of substantive law. This pressure is intense because of the large numbers of people that are involved and the profound social, economic, and public policy concerns that these new legal claims raise. The research of scientists working at the frontiers of human knowledge has become relevant in routine criminal cases; DNA testing, for example, has brought sophisticated science into the courtroom.

The growing prominence of science in the courtroom has exacerbated criticism of the courts' management and adjudication of S&T issues. Some allege that "junk science" is flooding the courtroom through the testimony of "experts," whose primary qualification is their willingness to testify in support of their client's position. As a result of these and similar concerns, there have been calls to remove certain categories of cases from the judicial system altogether. While some commentators believe that current legal procedures must be overhauled to deal with these abuses, others go even further in suggesting that the courts, dependent as they are on lay judges and juries, are incapable of properly resolving issues that turn on abstruse principles of epidemiology, toxicology, or statistics. Still others claim that the volume of litigation, as for instance in the cases arising from the use of asbestos, threatens the traditional model of individualized decision making. Given our judicial resources, it may be impossible to treat each case separately.

Our examination of the cases leads to the conclusion that, although such dissatisfaction does exist, many of the concerns expressed are greatly exaggerated. On the basis of reported decisions, it does not appear that the federal courts are being inundated with fringe science. Reported cases, of course, represent only the tip of the iceberg. The vast majority of cases terminate without opinion and without a trial, and there are few data available on how problems in handling S&T issues might have had an impact on settlements or discontinued suits. Misperceptions may become reality if settlements are driven by concerns about the courts' ability to reach consistent results. The Task Force's work to date and its recommendations, which seek to improve the system's ability to handle scientific evidence, should lead to better adjudications.

IMPROVING THE SYSTEM: NEW PROCEDURAL AND
EVIDENTIARY MECHANISMS, EDUCATION, AND
INSTITUTIONAL SUPPORT

Science is entering the courtroom more and more every day, and we believe that the courts' ability to handle S&T issues can be improved. Many of the tools to assist the judiciary already exist — it remains to encourage and assist judges to use them. Greater understanding of process, both the process of science and the process of managing complex evidence, is key to this endeavor. Accordingly, judicial education and the creation and dissemination of an S&T reference manual for judges are the twin pillars of our process recommendations.

The lack of institutional support for the judiciary must also be addressed when assessing ways to improve the courts' ability to resolve S&T issues. Unique among the branches of government, the judiciary has no ready recourse to outside assistance in its attempts to understand issues of science and technology. The Task Force believes that this situation can be ameliorated by creating more extensive and formal institutional ties between the S&T and judicial communities. These institutional recommendations, designed with the needs of the adversarial system in mind, should encourage increased dialogue between judges and scientists, to help scientists gain an understanding of the legal system and to assist judges in their understanding of the objectives and process of science.

THE FEDERAL JUDICIARY—OPPORTUNITY FOR INNOVATION

This is a particularly opportune moment to undertake an examination of judicial decision making on S&T matters in the federal judiciary and to suggest improvements. A sizable group of judges will undoubtedly be taking office within the year, so it is important to have S&T educational materials ready for incorporation into the initial judicial educational materials those new appointees will receive.

At the same time, new kinds of S&T cases are entering the courts in large numbers before science has adequately explored the issues involved. Recent developments, such as the FDA review of silicone implants, the allegations about repetitive stress injury, and the concern that cellular phones may cause brain tumors underscore the potential for the sudden emergence of new categories of mass tort cases. And any new mass tort boom is likely to fuel further public discontent with the judiciary's role in adjudicating S&T matters. Wisdom counsels action now.

MAJOR FINDINGS OF THE TASK FORCE

The Task Force's efforts to study the courts, which are discussed in more detail below, have yielded some new insights into the judicial system's treatment of S&T issues. In the course of its investigation, the Task Force considered the data that are currently available, reviewed the literature of legal commentators, held discussions with members of the legal and scientific communities, and commissioned new studies. In order to appreciate the rationale for the recommendations which follow, it is useful to review the Task Force's major findings:

LITIGATION PROCESS

- Although disparities abound in the way judges handle S&T issues, there is much less divergence in the actual results of cases. There is no one correct way of handling S&T evidence.

- Federal judges have adequate authority under the present Federal Rules of Civil Procedure and of Evidence to manage S&T issues effectively, and the rules of many state judicial systems are modeled on the federal rules.

- Increased attention to S&T issues at the pretrial stage makes cases more amenable to disposition by summary judgment, facilitates settlement, and leads to more focused, speedier trials.

- Expert testimony can be made more comprehensible to jurors.

- Judges and jurors may need information or assistance in handling S&T information that the parties cannot furnish because of insufficient expertise, mismatched resources, or excessive partisanship.

- Trial courts need guidance from appellate courts on the legal standards that control S&T issues.

JUDICIAL EDUCATION

- Because judges have little time available for judicial education, the challenge in designing an educational program is to produce materials on complex S&T issues to which a judge can turn when handling an analogous problem in an upcoming case. Thus, the ease with which judges can gain access to educational materials is as important as the quality of the materials.

- Appellate and trial judges and state and federal judges have differing educational needs that require different educational methods.

■ Science education programs, like all judicial education programs, are most effective if they are interactive, utilizing conversation, dialogue, and debate. Producing good-quality judicial S&T education programs requires the collaboration of lawyers who understand science and scientists who understand the needs of the courts.

■ The financial resources of the state and federal judiciaries are severely limited. While private foundations have funded the development of innovative education programs, they tend to withdraw support once the pilot program is completed. Funding for continuation even of those programs that have proven to be effective is rarely available.

RECOMMENDATIONS

■ Judges should take an active role in managing the presentation of science and technology issues in litigation whenever appropriate.

Many tools are available to state and federal judges to manage the presentation of S&T issues in litigation. The judicial reference manual and protocols, which are being developed by the Task Force in collaboration with the Federal Judicial Center, are two key elements of the effort to facilitate greater use of these tools.

The reference manual outlines the wide range of techniques that judges have used to manage S&T issues in litigation. It focuses on process and on the encouragement of judicial control. The manual presents judges with a range of options available to resolve a given issue and refers judges to S&T cases where those options have been used; it does not suggest substantive outcomes on contested science and technology issues.

Using the protocols, which are being developed jointly with members of the S&T community, will enable judges to identify and employ techniques that will permit quicker and more effective rulings on challenges to expert testimony, whether those challenges are based on the qualifications of experts, the validity of the theory on which the expert is relying, the reliability of the data underlying the theory, or the sufficiency of the expert's opinion to sustain a verdict.

In order to ensure that these tools continue to be useful, they must be updated systematically to reflect the most current scientific and legal developments. They will be even more valuable if references to state law are incorporated.

■ **Scientific and technical issues should be integrated into traditional judicial education programs, "modules" should be developed that can be appended to existing programs, and intensive programs should be supported.**

Judicial education programs play an important role in introducing judges to scientific methodology, which is an essential element in reducing misunderstandings about S&T evidence and in increasing judicial willingness to take an active role in managing that evidence. Because of the severe time constraints faced by judges, education about scientific methodology should be integrated into traditional judicial education programs. Existing judicial education programs should be expanded to include S&T "modules." For instance, a videotape could be produced that illustrates DNA analysis. Existing programs devoted exclusively to S&T issues should be identified, and others should be developed. These programs offer the greatest opportunity to give judges extensive, hands-on experience in dealing with the difficult S&T issues they may encounter in court.

■ **Institutional linkages between the judicial and scientific communities should be developed.**

Sustained improvement of judicial decision making on matters of science and technology requires the establishment of institutional ties to encourage greater dialogue and cooperation between the judicial and scientific communities.

■ The federal and state judiciaries should create S&T resource centers to provide judges with access to the collective experience of their colleagues in case management techniques for S&T issues and to educate judges on scientific methodology. Each resource center would also act as a clearinghouse for substantive scientific information compiled by the scientific community, monitor the impact of S&T issues on the courts, and serve as a bridge for cooperation with the scientific community. Each resource center should provide empirical data on the impact of S&T issues in various types of cases and use the results of that research to assist in long-range planning for the treatment of S&T issues in the judiciary.

■ The scientific community should create a resource center as a counterpart to the proposed judicial S&T resource centers in order to facilitate cooperation among the professional societies and to explore the benefits of continued interaction between the judicial and scientific communities.

■ A judicial S&T education clearinghouse should be established to collect and distribute curricula and other materials on science education for judges. An advisory committee of leading experts from various scientific disciplines, judicial educators, and representatives of the judiciary should be established to consider what judges need to know about science. It should also collaborate with academic communities in the fields of law and science to improve S&T programs and materials. The judicial S&T education clearinghouse should "package" high-quality science education programs for easy use and access.

■ An independent nongovernmental Science and Justice Council of lawyers, scientists, and others outside the judiciary should be established to monitor changes that may have an impact on the ability of the courts to manage and adjudicate S&T issues; it should also initiate improvements in the courts' access to and understanding of S&T information, including judicial education and communication between the judicial and scientific communities.

A continuing examination of the interaction between science and the courts is essential to efforts to improve judicial decision making concerning S&T issues. An interdisciplinary "Science and Justice Council" similar in mission to the Task Force should be created to continue the initiatives that the Task Force has begun.

Located outside existing institutions, the Council would be able to offer more strategic and long-range criticism and suggestions than existing groups with defined roles. The Science and Justice Council should also monitor changes in law, in science, and in society generally that may have an impact on the ability of courts to handle S&T issues.

Some judges are frustrated by their inability to obtain timely, nonadversarial explanations of the scientific and technical matters at issue in a case. Unlike the judiciary, when faced with unclear S&T information, Congress can consult the Office of Technology Assessment, and the Executive can consult the Office of Science and Technology Policy. The Council should undertake further study on the host of issues raised by the Task Force's proposal to create an institutional support mechanism for the judiciary, the form that such an advisory institution should take, sources of compensation for those providing assessments to the court, and permissible use of the information generated for the court.

Other areas that the Council might explore include data collection and alternatives to judicial resolution. Long-range efforts to improve the quality of judicial decision making with regard to S&T issues are hampered by the lack of adequate data about the incidence and management of scientific issues in the courts. Information is also necessary for appropriate allocation of judicial resources. In addition, little empirical information is currently available about the costs of handling S&T issues. And further study of how the judicial system copes with S&T issues and a comparison with administrative schemes such as the National Childhood Vaccine Injury Act would provide valuable information about the desirability and feasibility of pursuing the use of alternative forums.

We live in an ever-changing world to which a dynamic judicial system must be responsive. Unless reliable data are obtained so that changes can be anticipated, monitored, and evaluated, the ability of the courts to handle complex scientific and technological issues is compromised. The kinds of cases in which S&T issues occur are often those of the utmost social significance, and the decisions in them have major consequences for many people's lives. The way in which our society in general and the judiciary in particular will respond to the S&T issues of the future is of concern to many different constituencies whose views can best be heard, evaluated, and integrated at meetings of a broad-based heterogeneous group that is free of formal political ties. The Task Force believes, therefore, that it is important that an independent group, like the proposed Science and Justice Council, be created to monitor and develop further the recommendations outlined in this report.

CONCLUSION—A NOTE OF OPTIMISM

Unlike some recent critics, we end our survey of science in the courts on a note of optimism. The Task Force found that numerous innovative, highly motivated, and highly skilled judges and lawyers are working hard to improve judicial decision making with regard to S&T issues. That many problems remain is hardly remarkable, considering the magnitude of the legal and scientific issues that are presented to American courts for resolution. While the difficulty and novelty of the questions these cases pose preclude an instantaneous magical cure, we observe that the legal system is actively pursuing solutions.

Nevertheless, the Task Force believes that the handling of S&T evidence would be improved if more data were available on how the system works, if information about successful innovations were more widely disseminated, if judges were given more educational and institutional support, and if scientists, judges, and lawyers had greater opportunities to communicate with each other. At the moment, the parallel paths of scientists and lawyers usually obey the rules of Euclidian geometry—they do not intersect—even though both disciplines not infrequently ponder the same subjects. And when their paths do cross, the result is often misunderstanding, rather than constructive communication. At the very least, we hope that the Task Force's work will provide a starting point for a more fruitful interaction between the worlds of science and the law.

IDENTIFYING THE ISSUES

When science and technology enter the courtroom, they bring with them various problems. This chapter identifies and describes these difficulties; it also chronicles some of the principal steps that the Task Force took that culminated in the recommendations set out in Chapter 4. This report reflects the efforts of people actively engaged in the legal system, scientists from a variety of disciplines, policymakers and academics in a number of different fields. In its endeavor to improve judicial decision making with regard to scientific questions, the Task Force has also enlisted the assistance of federal governmental agencies such as the Federal Courts Study Committee and the Federal Judicial Center and has worked with state judicial systems through organizations such as the State Justice Institute and the National Center for State Courts.

Although this report refers to the judicial and scientific communities as if each were a discrete and homogeneous group of professionals, they are actually quite diverse and internally disparate (see "S&T and Judicial

---

S&T and Judicial Communities

The following descriptions of the scientific, engineering and judicial communities are not intended to be exhaustive or exclusionary. They are intended to reflect the diversity and complexity of the communities, which must be considered when contemplating interaction between them, whether during litigation, in education, or in other settings.

- The **S&T community** includes those engaged in the fields of mathematical sciences (mathematics and statistics), computer science, physical sciences (chemistry, astronomy, and physics), life sciences (agriculture, biology, medicine), environmental sciences (atmospheric sciences, earth science, oceanography), psychology, and social sciences (criminology, economics, geography, political science and government, sociology and anthropology). It also includes aeronautical, chemical, civil, electrical, industrial, materials, mechanical, mining, nuclear, petroleum, agriculture, computer, environmental, sanitary, marine, and systems engineers engaged in activities such as research, development, design, production, consulting, administration and management, teaching, technical writing, and technical sales or service.

- The **judicial community** consists of at least 53 independent systems, one federal, one for each state, and one each for the District of Columbia and Puerto Rico. Within each of these independent systems lie several autonomous levels of decision makers. In the federal system, there are 94 independent district courts and 13 appellate courts that comprise more than 700 trial judges and 150 appellate judges; all of these judges are appointed for life by the President with the advice and consent of the Senate. There are also tens of thousands of judges in state judiciaries. State judges are generally either elected or appointed for fixed terms of service.

    These numbers and characteristics do not begin to reflect the complexity of the relationships of the components of the judicial system in the United States. Several organizations represent various segments of the community, but the community is very much a collection of individual judges rather than a traditional pyramid-shaped bureaucracy. Every attorney is also an integral part of the judicial system, as each one takes an oath as an "officer of the court," with a measure of responsibility for its ability to function.

Communities," above). Much of the most vocal recent criticism and concern has been directed at the judicial system's response to evidence developed in the scientific community, but technological issues also cause problems for the courts. Engineers are among the most frequently encountered expert witnesses; they appear in a wide variety of cases such as construction disputes, product liability actions, and complex environmental litigation. Not surprisingly, the ever-increasing use of computers and electronic media is giving rise to many new issues in lawsuits. Future developments in bioengineering will also undoubtedly demand considerable judicial attention.

Complaints that expert testimony is too complicated, too costly, and too slanted surface regularly, whether the subject is science or technology. Consequently, although this report often uses the term "science," because public interest is currently focused on high-profile issues of "scientific" evidence such as the admissibility of DNA testing and the proof of causation in product liability litigation, in most instances the discussion is applicable to "technological" issues as well.

DISAGGREGATING THE PROBLEMS

Diagnosis was the first step before the Task Force could explore remedies for improving the use of science in litigation. Difficulties had to be identified and isolated before headway could be made in designing effective cures. Specific strategies were devised to investigate and target these questions:

- Are there reliable data about the types of scientific issues that arise in the judicial system, and about the frequency and severity of the problems they present?
- Is the judicial process seriously flawed because it relies on party-retained experts, who are perceived to be nothing more than hired guns, as the principal vehicle for introducing scientific evidence into court proceedings?
- Is the fact finder able to arrive at the "truth" despite the adversary system's exacerbation of differences between party-retained experts and the difference in the nature of "truth" in science and in law?
- Can judges and jurors who have no specialized scientific training comprehend the complex scientific evidence on which modern litigation sometimes turns?
- How can a court adequately inform itself when no viable mechanisms exist outside the adversarial process for supplying the court with input from the scientific community?
- Would institutional alternatives to the judiciary result in better, speedier, or less costly dispositions of science-related matters?

RESPONDING TO THE PERCEIVED PROBLEMS

Problems in judicial handling of S&T issues are clustered in four areas: the lack of data, the judicial system's procedures for handling expert testimony, the alleged inability of legal fact finders to grasp scientific knowledge, and the failure to make use of alternatives to judicial decision making when appropriate. An understanding of these areas is useful as a prelude to the more detailed discussions in the chapters that follow.

The Task Force carefully considered criticisms that the adversarial system itself is to blame for many of the problems in judicial decision making on scientific and technological matters. It concluded that this important subject requires further examination, including exploration of the possibility of removing entire categories of cases from the traditional system.

The Lack of Data

Knowledge about the impact of S&T issues on the courts is based on limited samples and extrapolation. Civil cases are typically classified by legal category, but these labels tell us little or nothing about the issues that are really in dispute. Furthermore, we have little data about the 90 percent of the federal cases that terminate short of trial, through mechanisms such as settlement, alternative dispute resolution, judicially decided motions, and dismissals for failure to prosecute. We do not know whether particular factors lead to these different results.

The ability to analyze or even describe what is happening in civil litigation is essentially nonexistent. Efforts at analysis are stymied by a lack of relevant statistical information. S&T issues, for example, occur in cases identified in court caseload statistics as contract, tort, statutory interpretation, and even constitutional law cases. Forensic advances, such as DNA testing, result in considerable S&T evidence being introduced in criminal trials as well.

One informal survey in the mid-1970s found that less than 3 percent of cases examined in the federal trial courts involved substantial S&T issues.[2] More recent data suggest a significantly larger percentage — perhaps as high as 20 to 30 percent.[3] Experts testified in 86 percent of civil jury trials that went to verdict, according to a recent study of California State Superior Court jury verdicts during 1985 and 1986.[4] While these data for California civil cases tried to verdict may not be representative of other jurisdictions, or of litigation generally, they do demonstrate that expert testimony about scientific and technological matters is already a significant issue for some courts.

Despite the paucity of specific information, we do know that those cases in the federal courts that involve scientific and technological issues, such as mass torts and environmental cases, present the judiciary with especially challenging problems. While they still account for only a small percentage of total caseload, the effort expended by courts in such cases is often disproportionately great: one experienced federal judge estimated that if the typical criminal case has a difficulty of 1, the typical case involving S&T issues would rank a 10, and a very complex S&T case might be a 30.[5]

Moreover, in the area of mass torts, the sheer number of cases raising science and technology issues can be staggeringly high: as of late 1991, there were approximately 30,000 asbestos cases pending in the federal courts, despite a drop of nearly 50 percent in new filings that year.[6] Similarly, the recent actions of the Food and Drug Administration concerning silicone gel breast implants have led some observers to predict extensive litigation from the more than 1 million American women who had received implants by January 1992. Others suggest that cases alleging repetitive motion injuries in the workplace will soon flood the courts.[7] New fears—such as the possibility that cellular phones can cause brain cancer—regularly provoke front-page news; the next step often is a lawsuit setting forth a novel scientific and legal claim.

More detailed, disaggregated data are needed to meet the challenges facing the judiciary today, particularly in the area of science and technology. Identification of the type of data that would be most useful for resource allocation, research on case management techniques, development of judicial education materials, and long-range planning is crucial. Yet changing or supplementing the current data collection systems is not a trivial matter. A significant investment of time, money, and goodwill is involved. A principal task of the judicial S&T resource centers proposed in Chapter 4 (see pages 49–61) would be to enhance the collection of data needed for empirical research and long-range planning.

THE DIFFICULTIES INHERENT IN THE JUDICIARY'S PROCEDURES FOR HANDLING EXPERT EVIDENCE

Party-retained experts have been denounced as hired guns ever since they first appeared at trials, long before complex scientific issues surfaced in litigation. Reliance on expertise managed by the litigants is, in part, a consequence of the adversarial system. Its effects are exacerbated by the lack of any resources within the judiciary that would aid judges to assess the relevant professional qualifications, the quality of professional societies and peer-reviewed journals in the discipline, and other factors. Consequently, judges are seriously handicapped in ruling on the admissibility of S&T evidence and in assisting the jury in their efforts to weigh an expert's testimony. An additional source of concern is the high cost of expert testimony even when the scientific issues are neither particularly complex nor novel. Fees for experts often add significantly to transaction costs that critics see as much too high.

Some blame the adversary system for encouraging each side to find less-than-neutral experts as witnesses and for tending to force party-selected experts into extreme positions that make settlement problematic and make it more difficult for the fact finder to evaluate scientific information. Courts often decline to exclude expert testimony or limit its scope. At the same time, the use of court-appointed experts to counteract the dangers of excessive reliance on party-selected experts is rarely utilized, even though "neutral" experts have been touted since the turn of the century by commentators such as Learned Hand.[8] Although all federal judges and many state judges currently have the option to appoint experts, a recent survey by the Federal Judicial Center found that only 20 percent of the federal judges responding had ever appointed an expert, and 52 percent of them had done so in only one case. Only one judge reported having appointed an expert in more than twenty cases.[9]

The problems that arise in the trial courts' handling of S&T issues also affect appellate courts. The reluctance of some appellate courts to provide detailed guidance on the relevant legal standards that will be applied to critical S&T issues (such as the requirements for a pretrial determination limiting or excluding proffered expert testimony) has hindered trial courts in disposing of issues expeditiously.

Rather than merely reiterating the various arguments that have been made about the present system's shortcomings in utilizing scientific evidence, the Task Force sought to reach the reality behind the rhetoric. After surveying the present patterns of expert proof in the courts, particularly within the federal system, the Task Force concluded that the development of specific evidentiary and procedural mechanisms can bring about improvement within the present adversarial system. Two of the Task Force's principal recommendations—a reference manual for judges and the development of protocols dealing with specific scientific issues (see pages 38–39)—are already being implemented. Furthermore, these initiatives are components of the Federal Judicial Center's pilot program (see page 54).

The Alleged Inability of Legal Fact Finders to Grasp Scientific Knowledge

Although the judicial system's ability to manage and adjudicate S&T issues can be enhanced, it is wishful thinking to imagine that all problems will vanish because the "truth" will emerge once the correct procedural approach is adopted. It is equally naive to believe that the scientific world can produce the "right" answer on request. Many S&T issues that are legally relevant because of the applicable substantive law raise the question of how to proceed in a world of imperfect knowledge. Lawyers and scientists approach uncertainty in ways that are characteristic of the goals their respective disciplines are seeking to achieve. In the courts, scientific knowledge must inform the choice, but abdication to the scientist is incompatible with the judge's responsibility to decide the law.

A Fundamental Difference

A fundamental difference distinguishes the task of judges from that of scientists. Our legal system authorizes aggrieved individuals to seek legal redress for their injuries. For example, when a plaintiff presents a claim of injury due to a silicone gel breast implant, the court is required to act, whether or not the scientific evidence is comprehensive or clear. It rarely has the option of dismissing or holding (staying) the case until scientists have had the opportunity to conduct in-depth studies. In this regard, the judge is more like an emergency room physician, who often must make decisions on a very incomplete medical record and with little information about the particular patient. In contrast, a scientist examining the question of whether silicone gel breast implants cause autoimmune diseases will continue to study the problem, design new experiments, and do more research.

This fundamental difference between judicial and scientific processes helps to explain some of the currently fashionable criticism of the judiciary for acting in the face of uncertain scientific evidence. In the absence of significant changes in substantive law, courts will continue to be faced with cases where the scientific evidence is uncertain or incomplete because the present state of science simply cannot give a definitive answer to the issues presented.

An Idealized View of Science

Critics of the judicial system's handling of scientific claims often have an idealized view of science that scientists themselves reject. Although these critics accept the indeterminacy of legal concepts, they speak of scientific "facts" as though they were objectively true, and they berate the legal system for failing to adduce conclusive evidence, even though scientists themselves concede that scientific hypotheses remain open to challenge until the incentives for attacking them disappear.[10]

While scientists are willing to acknowledge the contingent nature of scientific claims when speaking among themselves, they often react angrily when they appear as expert witnesses and hostile cross-examination exposes the assumptions that underlie their scientific claims. Scientists complain that any scientific consensus that does exist is obliterated in the adversarial attack. They contend that the legal system does not understand the answers that science has to offer—that many scientific facts are probabilistic statements based on theoretical assumptions and experimental traditions within a given scientific field. Rather than being asked to adduce personal opinions about absolute truth—did substance X cause disease Y?—the scientist would prefer to portray for the decision maker the range and distribution of prevailing scientific opinion.

The Burden of Proof in Science and Law

The reality is that courts often decide cases not on the scientific merits, but on concepts such as burden of proof that operate differently in the legal and scientific realms.[11] Scientists may misperceive these decisions as based on a misunderstanding of the science, when in actuality the decision may simply result from applying a different norm, one that, for the judiciary, is appropriate. Much, for instance, has been written about "junk science" in the courtroom. But judicial decisions that appear to be based on "bad" science may actually reflect the reality that the law requires a burden of proof, or confidence level, other than the 95 percent confidence level that is often used by scientists to reject the possibility that chance alone accounted for observed differences.

Inadequate Dialogue with Scientists

The Task Force concluded that some of the criticism of the judicial decision-making process is attributable to an inadequate dialogue between the legal and scientific communities, and an insufficient understanding of the differing cultures of law and science. Chapter 3 discusses in detail a variety of different projects aimed at informing the judicial and scientific communities about each other's methods and goals.

Inadequate Classification of Cases

The Task Force also believes that special management techniques for different categories of cases that involve S&T issues would result in more evidence being presented to the judge and jury that accurately reflects scientific propositions. The reference manual that is being prepared sorts cases according to two factors that appear most influential: (a) the extent to which S&T issues affect persons beyond the immediate parties to the litigation and (b) the extent to which the S&T issues are novel. When these factors are combined, three broad classes of cases emerge, each of which poses a central problem:

■ Routine, individualized effects cases, such as medical malpractice cases and routine personal injury actions, in which problems stem primarily from what is perceived as the excess partisanship of the expert witnesses

■ Cases that pose novel and complex S&T issues, such as toxic tort litigation or criminal cases in which a new forensic technique is offered, that will affect many like cases and that raise problems of scientific uncertainty

■ Cases in which the S&T issues are now mature, such as asbestos litigation, but where the problems caused by the huge numbers of litigants and issues may overwhelm the judicial system unless innovative techniques are used

Mechanisms designed to improve the quality of the S&T evidence that enters the legal system and to make the science more comprehensible are discussed in Chapter 2.

ALTERNATIVES TO JUDICIAL DECISION MAKING

Although S&T cases are in theory adjudicated within the traditional adversarial system, in practice they often are not. Caseload pressures and intensified judicial management promote settlements in all civil litigation. In the case of many mass torts, additional factors are at work. These cases are increasingly not treated as "normal" adversarial cases, either because they have been consolidated through multidistrict litigation and are subject to the special rules and procedures that apply to those cases, or because the sheer volume of those cases causes delay in their formal adjudication. Thus, formal, traditional adjudication by judges and juries through the adversarial process is more theoretical than actual in many of these cases.

The Task Force is well aware that in the last decade a number of studies have put forth proposals for removing certain controversies from the courts. The Task Force examined the studies of the ABA Commission on Mass Torts and the American Law Institute's Study on Enterprise Responsibility. The Task Force also considered the National Childhood Vaccination Injury Act as a possible statutory model for resolving compensation issues through administrative agencies. Although the Task Force does not have a recommendation that it wishes to make with regard to alternatives to judicial decision making, it recognizes the need to monitor future societal and legal developments so as to reassess periodically the desirability of retaining certain kinds of S&T cases in the courts, and to review alternatives. The independent nongovernmental Science and Justice Council that is proposed in the final recommendation in Chapter 4 (see pages 59–61) would provide an institutional mechanism that could support such investigations and initiatives.

FORMULATING A WORK PLAN

The Task Force took a multifaceted approach to examining and understanding judicial decision making on S&T issues. Disaggregating the bundle of problems, a work plan was developed to address the different facets. In the process, the Task Force worked closely with a number of institutions and individuals with special expertise in the area. The work plan and those collaborative efforts are described below.

FEDERAL COURTS STUDY COMMITTEE

At the time the Carnegie Commission commenced its work in 1988, systematic analyses or data gathering that focused on the actual performance of the courts in managing and adjudicating S&T issues had rarely been conducted in the federal or state systems. Fortuitously, the initiation of the Commission's work coincided with the launching of the Federal Courts Study Committee (FCSC), appointed by the Chief Justice of the United States at the direction of Congress to report on the federal courts of the United States.[12]

The Commission took the important first step of promptly contacting the FCSC. When the final report of the Federal Courts Study Committee appeared in April 1990,[13] it incorporated suggestions proposed by the Task Force. These included recommending a comprehensive examination of how courts handle complex S&T issues; consideration of procedural mechanisms for handling such issues; and exploration of ways to improve the ability of judges to comprehend S&T materials. The FCSC report also echoed the Task Force recommendation that the Federal Judicial Center (FJC) prepare a reference source to assist judges in managing cases involving S&T complexity.

Another important sign of the growing official awareness of the significance of S&T issues in adjudication occurred in May 1990. After considering the FCSC Report, the Judicial Conference of the United States recognized the increasing importance of economic, statistical, technological and natural and social science data in both routine and complex litigation, and called for research on the types of problems likely to be encountered in such cases and ways of handling them.[14]

FEDERAL JUDICIAL CENTER

The Task Force quickly sought to develop projects that would assist implementation of the FCSC and Judicial Conference recommendations. Interaction and cooperation with the Federal Judicial Center was viewed as fundamental in light of the Center's role within the federal judiciary as the focal point for research and education. Judge William W. Schwarzer, who became Director of the FJC in 1990, was invited to meetings of the Task Force and was kept apprised of its activities. What began as an informal interchange between the Task Force and the FJC has culminated in a pilot program within the FJC, funded by Carnegie Corporation of New York. The creation of this pilot program represents a recognition by the leadership of the judiciary of the need to place a high priority on improving the process by which S&T cases are adjudicated. This initiative, which is described in Chapter 4 (see page 54), provides an institutional base that will ensure the completion of ongoing projects begun by the Task Force.

Because the Task Force, from the outset, had placed a high priority on the reference manual, it first commissioned a report by Professor Margaret A. Berger that laid the groundwork for the reference manual by examining procedural and evidentiary mechanisms for dealing with S&T experts in toxic tort cases and making a number of recommendations for improving the process.[15] This report was distributed to all members of the federal judiciary and was favorably received. Professor Berger then began work on a comprehensive reference manual discussing the full range of topics related to the handling of S&T issues in the courtroom. That work is now well under way: several drafts have been reviewed by the Task Force, and the project has been endorsed by the Federal Judicial Center, which expects to issue the manual under its auspices upon completion sometime in 1993.

SCIENTIFIC COMMUNITY

The Task Force also sought the cooperation of the scientific community to assist judges in analyzing particularly troublesome S&T concepts often implicated in disputes over expert testimony. Papers on causation, toxicology, epidemiology, social science, and statistics were commissioned by the Task Force (see Appendix A). The Task Force also retained a number of scientist-lawyer teams to prepare model protocols for judges based on each consultant's paper. These protocols present a series of questions that seek to disaggregate the scientific and legal issues inherent in particular types of scientific or technical evidence. They provide the judge with a guide to current scientific and legal thinking about these issues but do not give advice on how the issues should be resolved. The Federal Judicial Center has agreed to collaborate in and extend the ongoing work of preparing protocols. An FJC-sponsored initiative has led to the completion of a protocol on DNA evidence.

OTHER ORGANIZATIONS

The Task Force also sponsored an effort to identify and recruit organizations for projects that would promote the improvement of judicial decision making with regard to S&T issues. A special subgroup of the ABA/AAAS National Committee of Lawyers and Scientists was convened to address the issues surrounding court-appointed S&T experts. The group submitted a report entitled "Enhancing the Availability of Reliable and Impartial Scientific and Technical Expertise to the Federal Courts," which recommended a demonstration project to explore means of matching scientific and technical expertise with the needs of the courts. The Commission is supporting the planning meeting for the demonstration project; the meeting will be held in 1993.

The Task Force has supported an Interbranch Symposium on Risk Management, which will be convened in 1993 at the Brookings Institution. The symposium is intended to further the recommendations of the Task Force for increased communication among the three branches of government on issues related to risk management.

At the Task Force's request, the RAND Institute for Civil Justice is preparing a model on the evaluation of mass tort litigation that identifies the various factors that distinguish mass torts from ordinary high-volume litigation, such as that dealing with automobile accidents.

The efforts of the Task Force to develop educational programs that will increase the scientific and legal communities' awareness of their differing methodologies and aspirations is the subject of Chapter 3.

Contacts of the Task Force staff with individuals and groups who are involved with S&T issues in judicial decision making have helped the Task Force immeasurably in its identification of issues and possible solutions. It is true that the lack of systematic data on the courts' handling of S&T issues somewhat obscures the landscape. But the significant markers that can be perceived through the ground fog made it possible to draw a map that we hope will be a useful guide to the salient issues with regard to science and technology in judicial decision making.

2

PROCEDURAL AND EVIDENTIARY MECHANISMS

A core component of the Task Force's effort to improve the adjudicative processing of S&T issues has been the identification of procedural and evidentiary mechanisms that promote the competent handling of S&T issues at various stages of litigation. A reference source for judges that describes effective case management techniques was from the first viewed as the appropriate end product of this effort. As discussed on page 30, the Federal Courts Study Committee endorsed this goal in its report of April 1990.

Initially, however, the Task Force recognized that it would be productive to examine closely the way in which the existing judicial system responds to science-laden cases. Studying the litigation settings in which S&T issues emerge enabled the Task Force to identify the problems that are causing the greatest difficulties for the legal system and to uncover flaws in existing procedural and evidentiary mechanisms. This analysis of current practice revealed the range of effective solutions currently available and allowed the Task Force to recommend ways of capitalizing on existing procedural and evidentiary mechanisms and to suggest improvements in the present system.

THE PROBLEMS

Science and technology issues pose serious challenges to trial and appellate courts. Not only do judges and juries face the difficulty of understanding complex scientific evidence, but judges bear the responsibility of managing the process by which this evidence is obtained and ultimately introduced into the litigation.

In order to discharge these responsibilities effectively, a judge in charge of a science-rich case may have to deal with abstruse information rooted in methodologies with which the court has little familiarity. Furthermore, the most troublesome cases in the judicial system are frequently those that turn on scientific issues that have not been definitively resolved or thoroughly examined in the scientific community. Since the judge ordinarily cannot defer decisions until more proof is available, cases that pose S&T issues may require policy choices about how to proceed in a world of imperfect knowledge and about who should bear the risk in the presence of uncertainty.

The judge's monumental methodological and jurisprudential task, which would be arduous under the best of circumstances, is further complicated by the ways in which scientific evidence is processed in our legal system. The Task Force focused on a number of frequently expressed concerns:

- Given current high settlement rates and the size of judicial dockets, is it worthwhile to invest scarce judicial time on S&T issues when the case is highly likely to terminate before trial?
- The information available to the judge is for the most part furnished by partisan witnesses selected by the parties. How can a scientifically naive court evaluate the qualifications of an expert as it must when a party moves to disqualify an opponent's expert? Faced with battling experts, how can a court rightly decide whether the expert's opinion is admissible in evidence? Is the court intruding on the role of the jury if it prevents expert testimony from being heard at trial? Does this process result in judicial opinions wanting in authority and consistency and jury verdicts at odds with "good" science?
- Litigation costs attributable to expert proof of S&T issues are inordinately high. If the judge wants more information or more assistance, will not litigation become even more expensive? If the costs of additional information are imposed on the parties, will less affluent litigants be driven out of the system? Are there cases in which the court should impose limits on acquiring S&T information? What is the relationship between more and better S&T information and increased delay?
- The information furnished by the parties' experts may be incomprehensible to the judge or may be devoid of certain details essential to

an understanding of the scientific issues. How can a court obtain help in understanding S&T information? Is it appropriate for a judge to seek additional information not furnished by the parties?

    ■ Long-existing mechanisms for utilizing court-appointed experts have rarely been exercised because judges are concerned about unduly influencing the jury, about identifying the need for an expert early enough in the process, and about locating and compensating an appropriate expert. Are other options available?

FINDINGS

The Task Force's efforts to study the courts through various initiatives discussed in this report have yielded many insights into the federal judicial system's treatment of S&T issues. Although we recognize the need for more accurate, specialized data about the prevalence of scientific evidence in the courts, much is ascertainable now about the federal judiciary's handling of scientific evidence.

    Many federal judges have written sophisticated and helpful opinions, commentary, and orders that can aid other judges in dealing with scientific evidence in court. Particularly in the last few years, legal commentators have supplied case studies as well as detailed critiques of the judicial response to important S&T issues, and recent reform efforts aimed at improving the rules of procedure and the rules of courts have described the operation of the present system in connection with suggestions for change. Based on these varied and extensive accounts and on work commissioned by the Task Force, a number of observations about the federal judicial system may be made:

■ *Recurring S&T problems — such as how to handle different types of proof of causation in toxic tort litigation — require courts to disentangle complex, intertwined legal and scientific issues.* One of the Task Force's objectives in the reference manual is to disaggregate the various questions courts consider when they deal with particular problems that are causing a good deal of difficulty. Judges will thus have ready access to legal and scientific authority with which to start their analyses.

■ *Although disparities abound in how judges handle S&T issues, there is much less divergence in the actual results in cases. Judges clearly approach the same problem in very different ways, but the seeming lack of uniformity and consistency is often superficial.* The ultimate outcomes with regard to highly complex scientific issues are remarkably consistent, at least within the federal system.[16] An objective of the recommendations in this report is to achieve more efficient and economic judicial resolutions.

■ *There is no one correct way of handling S&T evidence. Innovative, scientifically astute federal judges have developed a wide variety of effective, sophisticated techniques for managing S&T issues.* The Task Force's approach, embodied in the reference manual discussed later in this chapter, has been to suggest a menu of procedural and evidentiary mechanisms from which the judge can choose those items best suited to the particular needs of the case.

■ *A judge has adequate authority under the present Federal Rules of Civil Procedure and of Evidence to manage S&T issues effectively, and the rules of many state judicial systems are modeled on the federal rules.* Proposed amendments to the rules would require judges to take a more active role in the pretrial handling of expert witnesses. Even without these changes, however, individual judges can use techniques, and many do, that the amendments would make mandatory.

■ *Increased attention to S&T issues at the pretrial stage makes cases more amenable to disposition by summary judgment, facilitates settlement, and leads to more focused, speedier trials.* We recognize that the time a judge can devote to any one case is limited. However, active management of S&T issues will result in an ultimate saving of judicial time. Techniques exist to force the parties and their experts to produce more focused S&T information during discovery that will assist the court in identifying areas of agreement and issues requiring trial. The Task Force believes that confronting rather than ignoring problems with regard to an expert's qualifications, theory, or data often results in timelier, less costly dispositions. The protocols discussed later in this chapter will provide useful techniques to assist judges in this area.

We recognize, however, that judges have discretion with respect to the admission of relevant evidence and that they will therefore inevitably differ to some extent in their assessment of which issues must properly be left to a jury. Different approaches to screening expert testimony are in part a reflection of dissimilar jurisprudential attitudes as well as a consequence of disparate styles of advocacy and differences in the facts of the case.

■ *Techniques can be employed in conjunction with trial to make expert testimony more comprehensible to jurors.* A standard complaint is that jurors decide S&T issues by assessing the expert witness's demeanor instead of his or her expertise. To what extent this charge is true is difficult to document. It would seem, however, that excessive reliance on the expert's personality is much more likely if the jury is bewildered by the S&T proof and has no other means of judging its probative weight. The reference manual explores a number of ways to upgrade jurors' comprehension: improving the quality of the experts' testimony; highlighting for the jurors the issues on to which the experts agree and disagree; requiring the experts to testify seriatim; and providing more explanatory written materials, such as experts' reports, to the jurors. Furthermore, the judge's and jurors' comprehension could be improved before trial through tutorials conducted by the parties' experts. The use of court-appointed experts at trial is also considered.

■ *Judges and jurors may need information or assistance in handling S&T information that the parties cannot furnish because of insufficient expertise, mismatched resources, or excessive partisanship.* The present system authorizes the court to appoint experts to provide assistance, but courts have rarely availed themselves of this opportunity. Judges can use court-appointed experts in ways that would avoid some of the concerns that have inhibited courts from making such appointments on a more regular basis.

Court-appointed experts may be most useful when asked to report on particular, narrowly focused issues, and when they appear in connection with pretrial proceedings rather than at trial. Instead of providing another opinion about the ultimate issues in a case, the court-appointed expert might assist the judge in understanding the concepts that form the basis for the party-retained experts' opinions. The reference manual suggests how special masters can work in tandem with court-appointed experts to provide assistance to judges in framing questions. Other mechanisms for obtaining information and assistance from the scientific community must also be explored.

■ *Trial courts need guidance from appellate courts on the legal standards that control S&T issues.* For instance, must all scientific studies on which an expert relies meet the 95 percent confidence level that is often used by scientists to reject the possibility that chance alone accounted for observed differences? Is a lower standard compatible with the objectives of the preponderance of proof standard in civil litigation? How does a relative risk assessment interface with the applicable burden of proof? How should summary judgment motions be structured to ensure parties a reasonable opportunity to be heard? Now that the courts are more willing to grant summary judgment motions on the ground that plaintiff's expert proof is not admissible, adequate procedural safeguards are needed. Until such time as the Supreme Court deals with these legal issues,[17] the lower appellate courts must decide them. Consequently, additional support in the form of a reference manual, protocols, and educational programs may prove useful for appellate as well as trial courts.

JUDICIAL S&T REFERENCE MANUAL AND PROTOCOLS

Significant portions of the Task Force's recommendations are already being implemented. The establishment of a pilot program within the Federal Judicial Center ensures that work on the reference manual and protocols—two of the centerpieces of the Task Force's efforts—will continue.

REFERENCE MANUAL

The reference manual outlines the wide range of techniques that judges have used to manage S&T issues in litigation. It focuses on process and on the encouragement of judicial control rather than suggesting substantive outcomes on contested science and technology issues. To facilitate easy use by judges, the manual is organized thematically by litigation stages. It will alert judges to the wide range of options available for resolving a given issue and refer them to S&T cases where the various techniques have been used.

After the reference manual has been completed for the federal courts, it may be possible to add relevant state law references. Disseminating detailed blueprints to the judiciary about how S&T issues can be analyzed and managed accomplishes an important function. The reference manual should be helpful to judges who have not yet encountered particular S&T problems, as well as to judges who are interested in the approaches developed by other members of the judiciary.

PROTOCOLS

In addition to the manual, work will continue on protocols in the areas most frequently encountered by judges faced with S&T cases, such as toxicology, epidemiology, and (bio)statistics. These protocols, created jointly with members of the science and technology community, will provide suggested questions for judges that will permit quicker and more effective rulings on challenges to expert testimony, whether those challenges are based on the qualifications of experts, the validity of the theory on which the expert is relying, the reliability of the data underlying the theory, or the sufficiency of an expert's opinion to sustain a verdict.

Courts may not, for example, appreciate that the professional standing of scientists is based on such significant criteria as publication in certain peer-reviewed journals, the receipt of funding for research through a peer-review process, or the receipt of awards or acknowledgment from respected scientific organizations. Even though having or lacking such credentials may not be conclusive, information about these institutional mechanisms may offer some assistance to judges when ruling on threshold qualification issues.

As with the reference manual, the protocols must be systematically updated to reflect the most current scientific and legal developments, and additional protocols must be prepared. Once created, these protocols should be valuable to both federal and state judges. In addition, court orders and jury instructions that have been used in S&T cases should be collected and made available to judges.

OTHER INITIATIVES

In the course of its work, the Task Force identified a number of areas related to procedural and evidentiary issues that merit further study and examination.

DATA COLLECTION

There is a dearth of data about the incidence and management of scientific and technical issues in the courts. The crucial factors that determine outcomes must be classified, and the procedural and evidentiary response to S&T issues must be evaluated. Perhaps most important, such information will provide a valuable foundation for future planning. In the absence of good information about the magnitude of the problem, it is difficult to determine the appropriate allocation of resources. Furthermore, an early warning system could alert the judiciary to the appearance of a new claim that has the capacity to cause court congestion. Current examples are litigation involving breast implants and repetitive motion syndrome. Knowing when these types of cases enter the system would also provide researchers with the opportunity to conduct a detailed longitudinal study of the judicial system's treatment of the S&T issues.

The Task Force convened a discussion group of data collection experts to consider how to address these issues. The need for data collection is reflected in several of the recommendations in Chapter 4.

SCIENTIFIC ASSESSMENTS

Some judges feel hampered by their inability to obtain a nonadversarial explanation of the relevant scientific and technical issues. They also want critical studies and data early in the litigation cycle. Why should not judges be able to request assessments of the S&T matters at issue in a case, much as the Congress can consult the Office of Technology Assessment or the Executive can consult the Office of Science and Technology Policy? Research is needed on the form such an initiative should take, the mechanisms for making a request, sources of such studies and related compensation, and the various issues that would be raised by the availability of such assessments.

The Task Force convened a discussion group to consider the feasibility of such an assessment scheme. A recommendation on how to proceed is offered in Chapter 4 (see pages 59–61).

ALTERNATIVES TO JUDICIAL RESOLUTION

The Task Force recognizes the importance of monitoring the way in which the judicial system copes with S&T problems and of studying alternative mechanisms such as the administrative scheme established by the National Childhood Vaccination Injury Act. At this time, little empirical evidence is available about the costs in time and money of decision making with regard to S&T issues, regardless of the forum in question. Any such study must also consider the satisfaction of litigants with the justice they receive.

Recommendations about how these matters might be explored in the future are set forth in Chapter 4.

3

EDUCATION OF THE JUDICIAL AND SCIENTIFIC COMMUNITIES

Education is an important element in dispelling the misunderstandings and ignorance that impede improvements in judicial decision making with regard to science and technology issues. An educational effort must reach both scientists and judges in order to increase their familiarity with each other's expectations and methodology so that obstacles to the utilization of scientific information in legal proceedings can be overcome.

The Task Force's assessments, conclusions, and recommendations regarding judicial education rely significantly on the informal survey of science education programs for the state and federal judiciary that it undertook in 1992.[18] The purpose of the survey was to

■ Identify the states, judicial organizations, public institutions, universities, and federal agencies that offer educational programs on science, social science, and technology that are designed specifically to meet the needs of the judiciary.

- Review the substantive and procedural topics addressed in these programs.
- Determine who is being served by existing programs and whether it may be possible for a broader audience to benefit from existing programs.
- Identify individuals in the fields of science, social science, and technology who specialize in educating the judiciary on science and related topics.
- Evaluate various educational initiatives to determine which have the most promise for enhancing the ability of judges to manage and adjudicate cases involving complex scientific and technological issues.

This informal survey of programs offered in the past four years revealed that of the 800 science education programs and presentations, fewer than 100 actually dealt with scientific evidence and expert testimony. The vast majority of those offerings were developed to assist state trial judges. For the most part, faculty and presenters were drawn from the local area. The Task Force reviewed in greater detail twenty-five of the programs that had been commended for their in-depth examination of S&T issues, their reliance on the talent of scholars and experts in the relevant fields, and their ability to be replicated.

THE PROBLEMS

Two different but interrelated problems exist with regard to science in the courtroom that might be somewhat ameliorated by an educational initiative. First, lawyers and scientists do not adequately understand that law and science employ different methodologies even when investigating the same problem. Second, lawyers, including judges, generally lack scientific training. These deficiencies may lead to misunderstandings or to judicial reluctance to act.

PROBLEM-SOLVING: SCIENTIFIC AND LEGAL APPROACHES

In general, the method of scientific thinking is to develop hypotheses that will be critically examined. The agenda for this type of investigation is motivated by the research interests of the scientific community. Lawyers' approaches to problem-solving, on the other hand, are driven by the interests of their clients. They must determine precisely how a particular theory will operate in light of the specific conditions present in the case they are

DNA Evidence in the Courtroom

An example of how the legal and scientific approaches may clash is that of the recent introduction of DNA evidence in the courtroom. The general theory of DNA is unassailable. Lawyers do not question that, except for identical twins, every person's DNA is unique. For the lawyer, however, the introduction of DNA evidence at trials raised case-specific questions that science had never addressed, ranging over such issues as techniques for declaring a DNA match, the proficiency of examiners, laboratory control standards, and statistical problems. For instance, although it did not initially occur to scientists dealing with DNA under laboratory conditions to consider whether DNA samples can be degraded due to age or exposure to chemical or bacterial agents, lawyers raised these questions when the forensic sample was old or contaminated with other substances such as soil. As yet, little published research addresses these questions.

When lawyers pursued these issues in the courtroom, they were able to demonstrate sufficient problems in some instances to merit exclusion of the evidence. Some of the objections raised by lawyers have turned out to be groundless, while others have led to changes in the way DNA testing is done or have demonstrated the need for further scientific research.

The public, including some scientists, may not understand that these cases do not reject the underlying theory of the uniqueness of DNA. Rather, the facts of the particular cases required counsel to attempt to demonstrate that the conclusions drawn from the DNA evidence rested on covert assumptions that the scientific community had not yet articulated or tested.

Some scientists find disagreeable the courtroom ordeal in which their theories are deconstructed in public through the process of cross-examination. They may therefore refuse to participate in the judicial process. On the other hand, some lawyers express scorn for scientists who venture a conclusion without analyzing adequately all the assumptions on which that conclusion rests. They fail to realize that scientists in the laboratory need not pay heed to the individual factual settings that become relevant in litigation.

handling. While the scientist strives to construct and reach consensus, the lawyer has been trained to deconstruct his or her opponent's theory by demonstrating its inapplicability under the particular circumstances. The use of DNA evidence in the courtroom is a good example (see "DNA Evidence in the Courtroom," above).

An educational initiative that brings lawyers and scientists together to explore their different approaches, strengths, and weaknesses may lead to greater understanding and communication between the two groups. This, in turn, may foster greater participation by the scientific community in the adjudication of scientific issues and encourage a restructuring of some of the ways in which scientific issues enter the litigation process. For example, judges may begin to appreciate the extent to which the adversarial deconstruction process may make it more difficult to discern areas of scientific agreement. They may also recognize the value of utilizing innovative procedures in the pretrial stage that would narrow rather than widen the gap between party-retained experts. Similarly, scientists may be less disenchanted with the courtroom if they are more informed about the legal process.

LACK OF UNDERSTANDING COMPOUNDED BY LACK OF KNOWLEDGE

The problem of lack of understanding is compounded by lack of knowledge. Unease with scientific principles may lead judges to avoid analyzing cases that present S&T issues even though such cases could be disposed of on issues that require virtually no scientific understanding. There are cases, for instance, in which the expert testimony proffered simply does not fit the facts presented, and the court does not need to comprehend the expert's theory in order to make this determination. For example, an expert who concludes that plaintiff's disease was caused by product X on the basis of a study in which no one used product X should obviously not be permitted to testify. A judge uncomfortable with science may, however, be reluctant to address even a purely legal issue in a case that seemingly requires an understanding of theories of causation.

THE NEED FOR EDUCATION

Education becomes increasingly important as the system receives more and more cases that require judges to have some familiarity with scientific methodology and the factors scientists consider when they evaluate scientific work. Some comprehension of statistical and sampling concepts is crucial, given their importance in such disparate types of litigation as antitrust, discrimination, trademarks, and toxic torts. Also valuable would be some information about the operation of disciplines whose practitioners have only recently entered the courtroom, such as epidemiology and toxicology.

Education is therefore needed not only to acquaint the judicial and scientific communities with each other's methodologies and missions, but also to provide basic information. The protocols, discussed in Chapter 2 (see pages 38–39), that were commissioned by the Task Force and that will be continued by the Federal Judicial Center, may help provide some of this information and explain the scientific and legal context from which it emerges.

In examining S&T education for judges and scientists, the Task Force focused on the following challenges:

- Does judicial education usurp the role of the parties in educating the judge in a given case?

- How can judges or judicial educators identify effective S&T education programs or gain access to those programs that other judges have found to be most effective?

- Do the needs of state court judges differ from those on the federal bench? Are those needs being met by current programs?

- What are the needs of appellate courts for S&T education? Are those needs being met by current programs?

- How can S&T issues be most effectively communicated? Given the likely time lag between any formal program and a judge's encounter with a case posing S&T issues, are formal programs the most effective way to introduce judges to scientific methodology and sociology? How can judicial educators design effective, cost-efficient programs that utilize the lessons learned in handling science-rich litigation? How can judicial educators identify and secure the services of judges and scientists who are skilled at explaining scientific methodology?

- How can scientists become better acquainted with legal methodology and courtroom procedures? Would greater familiarity enable scientists to be more effective participants in the legal process?

FINDINGS

Like other areas involving S&T issues in the courts, judicial education is a realm where assumptions are rampant, but actual information is, as yet, rather scant. Thus, in addition to drawing on extensive discussions with judges and judicial educators and commissioned papers, the Task Force relied heavily on its survey of the existing science education programs for the state and federal judiciary in identifying the factors that matter most when designing an S&T educational effort for judges. The factors that form the basis for the Task Force's recommendations are set out below.

- *Judges are, by design, generalists who are unlikely to possess detailed knowledge of or familiarity with science and technology.* With the exception of some specialized courts such as the Claims Court of the United States, the selection of judges in the United States is not based on familiarity with S&T issues or methodology. For example, few newly appointed judges have experience with statistical analysis, which has become a critical element in an increasing number of cases. Not only are those named to the bench unlikely to have familiarity with S&T issues, but there is also no standard preparation for new judges to introduce them to these matters.

■ *Judges face extensive demands on their time, leaving little available for judicial education.* Moreover, many topics are competing for their attention, and they are unlikely to invest significant effort in a subject that they are not immediately confronting. In light of the severe time limitations faced by most judges, initial efforts to enhance education will be most effective if they focus on integrating science issues into traditional judicial education programs. Such integration provides the greatest opportunity to reach the greatest number of judges.

Although most educational efforts have been directed at judges in general, judges who know they must handle complex S&T issues in an upcoming case will seek more extensive information and assistance than is available in most current programs. For judges facing challenging S&T cases, S&T-specific courses can be very valuable. However, the length and expense of such programs means that they are unlikely to be utilized by a large number of judges.

■ *The ease with which judges gain access to educational materials is as important as the quality of the materials.* Access to effective judicial education programs is hampered by the lack of a clearinghouse for information about existing judicial education programs and materials. Replication of successful programs, or portions of successful programs, has proven to be very economical. Judicial education would be greatly enhanced if there were a centralized source with adequate resources to produce and make available high-quality S&T education materials. For example, there are some exemplary programs that have been developed by universities, but judges, judicial educators, and academics in other regions have no way to learn about these programs. Although the Federal Judicial Center is taking a more active role in developing S&T materials for inclusion in its programs, efforts need to be undertaken to develop a suitable entity to take on this important clearinghouse function.

■ *Although many S&T issues involve ethical and moral considerations, little attention is paid to such matters in most judicial education programs.* More and more often, judges are being called upon to make legal and moral decisions that will dictate the quality and meaning of life, as they decide issues relating to birth, the right to die, and the allocation of scarce medical resources. Judges might welcome the opportunity for education that addresses the scientific and philosophical complexities that bear on making such decisions.

■ *Appellate and trial judges and state and federal judges may have differing educational needs and may require different educational methods.* Virtually all of the present programs are directed towards the needs of trial judges. Little if any attention has been paid to the particular needs of appellate judges, such as understanding risk assessment for review of agency actions. Federal and state judges may also have somewhat varying needs stemming from differences in their caseloads.

■ *High-quality judicial S&T programs require collaboration by judges who understand science and scientists who understand the needs of judges.* Many of the programs that judges have found most useful were designed with the active assistance of teams of judges and scientists who are skilled at providing "interpretation" of the other culture's language and methodology. Judicial education programs that feature subject-matter experts with little knowledge of the judiciary or the judicial system are often "interesting," but judges may leave feeling that they have wasted precious time if they cannot apply "on the bench" what they have learned.

■ *Science education programs, like all judicial education programs, are most effective if they are interactive, utilizing conversation, dialogue, and debate.* Adult education theory has shown that people are most likely to retain material if they acquire it in an interactive process. The anecdotal reports from judges on current judicial education programs reveal that they believe the "hands-on" programs to be most useful. It appears that effective judicial education programs

■ Focus on scientific methods rather than substantive science, with opportunities for judges to practice "hands-on" application of scientific methods and theory in a judicial context

■ Include problem-solving exercises to help judges understand how scientists think

■ Include interactive presentations such as workshops or mock trials, as contrasted with lectures, to explain differences between scientific and legal concepts

■ Make available, before and during educational programs, clear and useful resource materials, including protocols designed to assist judges in addressing issues of expert testimony (see pages 38–39)

■ Include presentations by members of the judiciary who are experienced in trying cases involving S&T issues, as well as simulations involving lawyers and experts

■ Include sufficient time for discussion among the participating judges of issues raised by the presentations and simulations

The Task Force and the Federal Judicial Center are engaged in designing a pilot program applying these principles in the United States District Court for the Eastern District of New York. We are hopeful that this initiative will provide a blueprint for future efforts.

■ *The financial resources of the state and federal judiciaries are severely limited.* The primary barriers to reaching greater numbers of federal and state judges are time and money. Although on the federal level the Federal Judicial Center has been successful in obtaining increased funding for judicial education, the number of judges to be served has risen substantially, and there is greater competition for the Center's limited resources and attention. Many state judicial budgets have been cut, making development of and participation in judicial education programs more difficult. The primary source of outside funding for state judicial education, the State Justice Institute, can support only a fraction of the proposals it receives each year.

Private sources of funding, particularly corporate sources, are necessarily limited by concerns about conflicts of interest. Private foundations have funded the development of innovative education programs; however, even where those programs are effective, foundations tend to cease funding once the pilot program is completed. This reality has significant implications for the kinds of programs that can be undertaken as well as for the types of institutions that are best suited to undertake development of educational programs.

Recommendations for enhancing educational initiatives are set forth in Chapter 4.

4
RECOMMENDATIONS

The Task Force proposes four distinct but interrelated initiatives for improving the quality of scientific and technological information that enters the courtroom and for enhancing the ability of judges to manage and adjudicate the cases in which this information is relevant.

- Judges should engage in the active management of complex S&T issues throughout the stages of litigation whenever appropriate.
- Judicial education should include S&T issues, both in programs of a general nature and in focused S&T programs.
- Institutional linkages should be forged between the judicial and scientific communities.
- A Science and Justice Council, consisting of lawyers, scientists, and others outside the judiciary should be established to initiate and monitor developments and to suggest future reforms with respect to the judicial system's treatment of scientific and technological issues.

The Task Force's detailed recommendations follow.

AN ACTIVE ROLE FOR JUDGES

■ Judges should take an active role in managing the presentation of science and technology issues in litigation whenever appropriate.

The findings of the Task Force, outlined in Chapter 2, with regard to the operation of evidentiary and procedural mechanisms in the current system support an active role for judges confronted with S&T issues. The Task Force's efforts and commissioned studies have led it to conclude that although there is no one correct way to handle S&T evidence, active involvement by the judge at various stages of the litigation may lead to better, less costly, and quicker resolutions.

This conclusion recognizes that the precise time when the judge should take measures will depend on the characteristics of the particular case. Generally speaking, however, earlier hands-on management by the court may ultimately result in savings for the litigants. Case management techniques exist that are specifically geared to the differing problems that various kinds of cases present with regard to S&T issues at particular stages of litigation.

This recommendation takes into account the possibility that a judge may be reluctant to spend scarce judicial time on complex S&T issues until it is clear that attention to these issues will advance the disposition of a case. We believe, however, that without undue investment of time, a judge's active management of S&T issues can help ensure that

■ The parties will produce better and more focused S&T information at the discovery stage.

■ The party-retained experts will narrow their areas of disagreement.

■ In appropriate cases needed assistance can be obtained from magistrate judges, court-appointed experts, or special masters.

Experience shows that it is constructive for the judge to take early action to prevent testimony from an unqualified witness, or testimony that does not meet applicable standards of admissibility. Such action, of course, is appropriate only if the parties are provided with an opportunity to be heard. And disposition of a case by the court before trial or at trial is possible in a jury-triable matter only if the court can conclude that no reasonable juror could make a determination in favor of the plaintiff or defendant on the basis of the proffered evidence. More active management is worthwhile, however, even when the court cannot dispose of a case: the judge's efforts may produce a more narrowly focused, speedier trial that is more comprehensible to the jurors and that allows them to reach results that reflect S&T evidence more appropriately.

The judicial reference manual will provide judges with a menu of options from which to select methods for handling particular S&T problems in a variety of cases. Work is also continuing on the protocols discussed in Chapter 2 (pages 38–39).

INTEGRATION OF S&T INTO JUDICIAL EDUCATION PROGRAMS

■ **Scientific and technical issues should be integrated into traditional judicial educational programs, "modules" should be developed that can be appended to existing programs, and intensive programs should be supported.**

Chapter 3 discusses the need for educational programs that improve the judge's understanding of scientific methodology and that explain basic scientific and statistical principles. This is a particularly opportune moment for undertaking a major educational initiative because more than a hundred vacancies currently exist in the federal courts. An effort should be made to incorporate scientific issues into the training programs that will be offered to new judges.

It is obviously impossible to provide judges with the equivalent of a specialized scientific education in all or even any of the disciplines that may be relevant in a particular case. Because lawyers are trained to use information in legally relevant situations, programs that consider scientific issues in the context of cases typical of those a court is likely to encounter are more effective than lectures about science.

In light of the severe time constraints most judges face, educational efforts should as a first step integrate science into traditional judicial education programs. For instance, a program on summary judgment could use a science-based dispute as an example. While the central focus of the program would be on the summary judgment process, the problem would require consideration of whether a particular scientist's expert testimony is admissible, or whether the plaintiff's expert proof *in toto* is sufficient. Integrating S&T issues into general programs is a way to raise a judge's awareness about different possible approaches, new cases, and new issues. Although this approach can be targeted to reach a great number of judges, it is unlikely to provide them with much detailed assistance in handling any scientific problem in depth.

"Modules" of educational material on science-based information can be quite effective when added to existing programs if they are well packaged and presented. They can give the judge a greater understanding of scientific methodology, or some assistance with a narrow technical question, without demanding an extraordinary commitment of time. For instance, a tape could show and explain what DNA evidence looks like, or demonstrate sampling techniques, or illustrate various formulas statisticians use in discrimination cases.

Efforts also must be made to identify existing programs devoted exclusively to S&T issues and to develop new ones. These programs offer the greatest opportunity to engage judges in extensive, hands-on experience in dealing with the difficult science and technology issues they might encounter in court. For judges facing challenging S&T cases, such courses can be very valuable. However, because of the time and expense entailed in attending such programs, they are unlikely to be utilized by a large number of judges. It may, however, be possible to videotape some of these programs and make relevant sections available to the judge in chambers. Simulations are particularly effective because they can be used to present crucial issues realistically and dramatically. If at all possible, they should be prepared in a reusable format, such as videotapes or computer programs.

LINKAGES BETWEEN THE JUDICIAL AND SCIENTIFIC COMMUNITIES

■ **Institutional linkages between the judicial and scientific communities should be developed.**

As discussed throughout this report, a central difficulty is that lawyers and scientists do not understand each other's disciplines very well. This cultural gap is aggravated by the lack of institutional linkages between the judicial and scientific communities. The absence of institutional ties leads to misunderstandings about language, methodologies, and missions that often have a surface similarity. Furthermore, the lack of affiliation means that the judiciary does not have a group of scientists to which it can turn for institutional support. In contrast, the executive and legislative branches of the federal government have ready access to a broad spectrum of information through federally funded think tanks, in-house science advisors, and the congressional Office of Technology Assessment.

Many of the initiatives to improve judicial treatment of S&T issues require greater cooperation among existing institutions and, in some cases, either the creation of new entities to facilitate linkages or the shouldering of new responsibilities by existing institutions.

Historically, no institutional entity has been responsible for overseeing or managing the interaction between science and the law. From the beginning of its efforts, the Task Force sought to improve the judicial treatment of S&T issues by creating more formal institutional ties between the judiciary and the scientific community. The Task Force was instrumental in the establishment of a S&T resource center within the federal judiciary (see "Federal Judicial Center S&T Resource Center Project," page 54). It also encouraged the scientific and technical community to establish more formal lines of communication with the judiciary (see "Establishing a Link with the Scientific Community," page 55).

An effective way to enhance the institutional capability of the courts to obtain and understand scientific and technological information is to create science and technology resource centers in both the state and federal judiciaries to address scientific issues that arise repeatedly in adjudication. An analogous resource center should be created in the science community to facilitate communication with and understanding of the judicial community. These centers should be designed to reflect the interests of the judicial and scientific communities and to bridge institutional gaps without compromising the independence or vitality of either group. They should also serve as catalysts and facilitators, drawing on the expertise of the relevant communities and organizations.

JUDICIAL S&T RESOURCE CENTERS

■ The federal and state judiciaries should create S&T resource centers to provide judges with access to the collective experience of their colleagues in case management techniques for S&T issues and to educate judges on scientific methodology. Each resource center would also act as a clearinghouse for substantive scientific information compiled by the scientific community, monitor the impact of S&T issues on the courts, and serve as a bridge for more cooperation with the scientific community.

Chapter 2 describes the ongoing effort to develop protocols designed to assist judges in dealing with particular scientific issues and to develop a reference manual that advises judges of procedural and evidentiary mechanisms that can be used to handle S&T issues effectively. A judicial S&T resource center could usefully undertake the further production, updating, and dissemination of protocols and the reference manual, and, indeed, the Federal

Federal Judicial Center S&T Resource Center Project

In 1990, the Task Force endorsed the concept of a resource center for S&T issues within the judiciary. Consultants were retained to explore the activities such a center should undertake to facilitate communication of timely and relevant information. At the same time, the Task Force began discussions with the Federal Judicial Center to explore ways in which the FJC could play a role in such a proposed resource center. (The Task Force and the FJC were already engaged in cooperative efforts to develop a judicial reference manual for procedural guidance in the management of scientific and technical issues, as well as a draft protocol on DNA evidence.)

In the summer of 1992, the Federal Judicial Center's Board of Directors approved a proposal by Judge William W. Schwarzer, the director of the FJC, to launch a 3-year pilot project on judicial management of scientific and technological evidence. The proposal was developed with the active encouragement of the Task Force. The project is designed to

- Prepare and maintain a science and technology manual for federal judges
- Develop science and technology components for judicial education programs
- Identify needed research and planning to improve the judiciary's ability to handle scientific and technological information
- Engage in outreach and liaison with the scientific and technical communities

Carnegie Corporation of New York has funded the pilot project through the Federal Judicial Center Foundation. Work has begun on several initiatives, most notably on the production of the reference manual and protocols, which are discussed at length in Chapter 2. The willingness of the FJC to establish such an S&T center on a trial basis demonstrates both the feasibility and the desirability of establishing resource centers within organizations that already exist in judicial systems. Because of its able staff's expertise in related areas, the FJC was able to begin work on these projects immediately.

Judicial Center has indicated its intention to continue these efforts. Regular updating and dissemination are essential because of the changing nature of S&T issues the courts will face over time, and because effective new techniques will become available as time passes. Maintenance of these vital documents should be a high priority of the S&T resource centers, lest the collective wisdom, experience, and expertise of those involved in the adjudication of S&T issues become outdated and therefore irrelevant to new generations of judges.

Establishing a Link with the Scientific Community

The Task Force has encouraged and supported a project of the ABA/AAAS National Conference of Lawyers and Scientists to develop mechanisms that would enable the scientific community to identify potential expert witnesses for the judiciary. It has also engaged in informal discussions with the National Academy of Sciences to explore ways in which the scientific community could assist the judiciary in better understanding S&T issues, as well as ways of educating scientists about how the judicial process works. Although still quite preliminary, these efforts may provide a foundation for establishing more formal relationships in the future.

■ *The judicial S&T resource centers should provide empirical data on the impact of S&T issues in various types of cases.* Data are needed to reveal the impact of S&T issues on litigation, to warn of impending difficulties, and to take advantage of innovative approaches to judicial treatment of S&T issues. The centers should design systems to collect, analyze, and disseminate court data on the number, type, and attributes of cases involving significant science and technology issues. As noted in Chapter 1, traditional court statistics have not been compiled in a manner that identifies the presence of any substantial S&T issue. As a result, accurate information on how frequently these issues arise and on their impact upon the courts is currently unavailable.

■ *The judicial S&T resource centers should use the results of that research to assist in long-range planning for the treatment of S&T issues in the judiciary.* There is a growing consensus that long-range planning is needed in the judiciary,[19] especially in the area of S&T issues. Long-range planning efforts in the judiciary have been hampered by the lack of empirical research on science and technology issues in the courts; when unplanned for, some cases, such as asbestos litigation, have the capacity to overwhelm the system. The data collected by the proposed centers will help to overcome this historical barrier. With more accurate data about trends in science and technology issues in the courts, the judiciary will be better able to anticipate substantial new claims put forth in litigation, such as those stemming from silicone breast implants, lead poisoning, or repetitive motion injuries. Although courts are necessarily reactive, timelier awareness of emerging large-scale problems will permit the earlier design, preparation, and dissemination of targeted educational materials and the early use of innovative case management approaches.

- *The judicial S&T resource centers should explore ways in which continued interaction between the legal and scientific communities will be beneficial.* The resource centers might host meetings between scientists and judges; convene seminars for leaders in the national academies, professional societies, and judicial communities; distribute materials developed by the S&T communities to the state and federal judicial and legal communities; and consider the possibility of developing registers of qualified scientists who could assist judges as court-appointed masters or experts. Once such cooperative efforts are begun, the two communities may find other ways to diminish obstacles to more effective management of S&T issues in litigation.

S&T Resource Center in the Scientific Community

- **The scientific community should create a resource center as a counterpart to the proposed judicial S&T resource centers in order to facilitate cooperation among the professional societies and to explore the benefits of continued interaction between the judicial and scientific communities.**

A healthy, ongoing dialogue needs to be established between the judiciary and the S&T community. This dialogue would be greatly enhanced by the creation of a S&T judicial resource center in the scientific community; this center should be linked with the judicial resource centers. Such a resource center in the scientific community should assist the state and federal judiciaries in the development of educational materials, assist with the preparation of information about S&T expert qualifications, provide lists of potential experts upon request, and provide substantive information on S&T issues.

The scientific resource center should also assist scientists in better understanding legal methodology and the judicial decision making process and help S&T professional associations to encourage their members to become more active participants in the judicial process. Scientific societies have indicated their willingness to offer educational or other assistance.[20]

Particularly helpful to courts would be reliable statements identifying the elements of acceptable scientific methods field by field. For example, such a statement would identify the factors an epidemiologist would consider in determining whether an epidemiological study had been properly conducted. An ongoing dialogue between the judiciary and S&T communities would ensure that these efforts are coordinated with the needs of the judiciary. The possibility of drafting ethical codes for expert witnesses in various disciplines should also be explored.

Judicial S&T Education Clearinghouse

- **A judicial S&T education clearinghouse should be established to collect and distribute curricula and other materials on science education for judges.**

Although effective judicial education programs on judging science exist, there is unintentional duplication of judicial education programs in S&T, producing higher costs for the judiciary and materials inferior to those that could be produced by a coordinated effort. A judicial S&T resource center might perform clearinghouse functions, such as

- Gathering curricula and resource materials designed to assist the judiciary in understanding and adjudicating complex S&T scientific issues
- Gathering materials from exemplary science education programs and making those materials available to judicial educators and other judicial personnel
- Identifying topics that are not being addressed by judicial education programs and developing educational curricula and resource materials that clarify these topics
- Identifying a "cadre" of judges and scientists who can advise those designing judicial S&T education programs and who can assist in integrating science examples into traditional judicial education programs

- *The judicial S&T education clearinghouse should establish an advisory committee of leading experts from various scientific disciplines, judicial educators, and representatives of the judiciary to consider and advise about what judges need to know about science.* The advisory committee's primary task would be long-range planning that would attempt to incorporate relevant developments in S&T into judicial education programs. Successful judicial education programs address not only "what judges know they don't know," but also "what judges *don't* know they don't know." In addition, the advisory committee should identify any areas in which the judiciary's education needs are not now being met. For instance, it may be desirable to develop a curriculum tailored to the distinct needs of the appellate courts. The advisory committee should also consider the most appropriate way to include ethical and moral considerations in judicial education on science and technology.

- *The judicial S&T education clearinghouse should also collaborate with academic communities in the fields of law and science to improve S&T programs and materials.* Many of the best science and technology judicial education programs in the country are sponsored by universities and law schools.

Judicial Education Resource Packages

The judicial S&T resource packages should include

- Curriculum with modules that could be presented together or separately
- Suggestions for successful approaches to teaching a particular module, including explanations of problem-solving exercises that have proven successful in previous programs
- Lists of readings and other resource materials to be distributed before a conference or program, including case studies, annotated case summaries, and recent opinions
- Expert depositions and motions as well as sample motions from opposing parties
- Packaged slide presentations or copies of films that have been used by other judicial educators
- Clear explanations of procedural approaches and analyses of previous successful (or unsuccessful) approaches in representative complex cases
- A list of resource people—scientists and judges who have taught together in the past or who have a special understanding of the issues involved—who might serve as faculty or advisors
- A list of judicial education programs in other states or localities that addressed the same topic, with names of individuals to contact for more information

These programs and conferences, which range from one-day seminars to multisummer degree programs, offer a wealth of information and talent.

The establishment of more formal relationships between federal, national, and state judicial education programs and law schools and universities that have developed programs in law, science, and technology could substantially improve the quality of judicial S&T education.[21] More formal ties would afford the judiciary more input into these programs so that they better meet the specific needs of judges.

The goal would be to create a network of law professors and reputable scientists from academia, industry, and government who are skilled teachers, who understand the judiciary, and who can apply their knowledge in a judicial context. This network would constitute a valuable resource for judicial educators attempting to design programs for judges. Greater cooperation between judicial educators and academic institutions might also encourage changes in the law school curriculum to educate law students about scientific and statistical issues that they are likely to encounter in their future professional lives.

■ *The judicial S&T education clearinghouse should "package" high-quality science education programs for easy use and access.* Resources should be targeted for group programs and presentations as well as for programs to be used by individual judges. The ease with which the judges can gain access to educational materials is as important as the quality of the materials. Replication of existing programs through the development of resource packages would be economical and would provide a rich educational experience to greater numbers of judges. Resource packages should include all of the material necessary for producing a quality program (see "Judicial Education Resource Packages," page 58).

With greater use of packaged materials that draw on the experience and expertise of many, it should be possible to make this particularly effective teaching tool available to more judges. Packages should also include resource lists of other materials that would be suitable for use by an individual judge. Every effort should be made to have materials available through on-line computer services. Computer-accessible materials would be available in a timely and inexpensive manner to judges and judicial educators throughout the country. Wherever feasible, such a package should also include interactive video disks and tapes, or at least information indicating that such interactive tools exist.

SCIENCE AND JUSTICE COUNCIL

■ **An independent nongovernmental Science and Justice Council of judges, lawyers, scientists, and others should be established to monitor changes that may have an impact on the ability of the courts to manage and adjudicate S&T issues; it should also initiate improvements in the courts' access to and understanding of S&T information, including judicial education and communication between the judicial and scientific communities.**

The deliberations of the Task Force over the past three years have made it increasingly evident that efforts to improve judicial decision making with regard to S&T issues must continue beyond the life of the Task Force. The kinds of cases that involve complex scientific and technological evidence seem to be on the increase. Furthermore, these cases often raise critical issues of social and economic policy, since they turn on who should bear the risk of the scientific and technological innovations that generally enhance our lives but that may also cause problems. To improve the judicial system's ability to deal with these difficult questions, a continuing effort to increase the interaction between science and the courts is essential.

The Task Force's experience confirms that an independent, broad-based group can play a unique role in proposing new ideas for improving judicial decision making with regard to S&T issues. A similar type of interdisciplinary council should continue the initiatives the Task Force has begun. It should consist of judges, lawyers, scientific and technological experts, academics, and perhaps members from industry and the other branches of government.

An important characteristic of the proposed council is that it would be located outside existing institutions and therefore would be freer to offer strategic and long-range criticisms and suggestions than existing groups with defined roles. The proposed council could, for instance, explore the feasibility of mechanisms which would enable a court to obtain needed scientific information. When a new type of claim enters the court system, as is happening with breast implants and as may occur with electromagnetic fields, judges may want information based on existing studies, ongoing research, or governmental investigations. At this time, there is no formal way in which a court can seek this information. The council might propose legislation, or court rules, that would enable a court, perhaps through the Judicial Conference of the United States, to certify requests for information to administrative agencies or private bodies within the scientific community.

Such a council could also make recommendations about curricular change in our nation's colleges and law schools. It has been suggested, for instance, that a working knowledge of statistics is becoming so important for lawyers that a course in statistics should be required either as a prerequisite to law school admission or for graduation from law school. At the very least, law schools should be encouraged to offer elective courses in Law and Statistics, as some leading law schools now do. The council could explore these various options and could consider as well the kinds of statistical courses that would be most helpful to practicing lawyers.

We live in an ever-changing world to which a dynamic judicial system responds. The council should monitor changes in the law, in science, and in society generally that may have an impact on the ability of the courts to handle S&T issues. We recognize that even as this report is being written, events are taking place that may have a profound effect on how S&T issues are handled in the courts. On the immediate legal horizon are proposed changes in procedural rules, a Supreme Court case on the standards of admissibility for scientific evidence, and the American Law Institute's new Restatement (Third) of Torts: Products Liability, as well as proposed new mechanisms that would permit the consolidation of cases on a massive scale. New scientific research efforts may produce results that will affect many of the issues currently before the courts. And, of course, the legislative and executive branches may undertake initiatives with major impact on the courts.

Unless these changes are monitored, it is virtually impossible to evaluate the ability of the courts to handle these complex scientific and technological issues. The kinds of case in which these S&T issues arise are often those of the utmost social significance, and the decisions of judges and jurors have major consequences for many peoples' lives. A group that initiates and monitors change in the legal arena and is aware of the complicated interrelationships within and outside the legal system would be able to evaluate recommendations and to propose solutions for these pressing problems. We believe, therefore, that it is important that an interdisciplinary, nonpolitically affiliated group monitor the performance of the judicial system to evaluate its ability to cope with these problems.

CONCLUSION

Unlike some recent critics, we end our survey of science in the courts on a note of optimism. The Task Force found that numerous innovative, highly motivated, and highly skilled judges and lawyers are working hard to improve judicial decision making with regard to S&T issues. That many problems remain is hardly remarkable, considering the magnitude of the legal and scientific issues that are presented to American courts for resolution. While the difficulty and novelty of the questions these cases pose preclude an instantaneous magical cure, we observe that the legal system is actively pursuing solutions.

Nevertheless, the Task Force believes that the handling of S&T evidence would be improved if more data were available on how the system works, if information about successful innovations were more widely disseminated, if judges were given more educational and institutional support, and if scientists, judges, and lawyers had greater opportunities to communicate with each other. At the moment, the parallel paths of scientists and lawyers usually obey the rules of Euclidian geometry — they do not intersect — even though both disciplines not infrequently ponder the same subjects. And when their paths do cross, the result is often misunderstanding, rather than constructive communication. At the very least, we hope that the Task Force's work will provide a starting point for a more fruitful interaction between the worlds of science and the law.

APPENDIXES

APPENDIX A
PAPERS PREPARED FOR THE TASK FORCE

Except as noted, these papers are unpublished.

AAAS-ABA National Conference of Lawyers and Scientists Task Force on Science and Technology in the Courts, "Enhancing the Availability of Reliable and Impartial Scientific and Technical Expertise to the Federal Courts" (1991).

Linda Bailey, "Protocol for Epidemiology" (1992).

Margaret A. Berger, *Procedural and Evidentiary Mechanisms for Dealing with Experts in Toxic Tort Litigation: A Critique and Proposal* (1991; Carnegie Commission on Science, Technology, and Government).

Troyen A. Brennan, "Legal Evidence of Toxic Causation" (1990).

Edward Burger, Jr., "Outline of a Series of Issues Raised by the Adjudication of Scientific Complex Cases" (1989).

Edward Burger, Jr., "Judicial Education and S&T Resources for the Courts" (1989).

E. Donald Elliott, "Issues of Science and Technology Facing the Federal Courts" (1989).

Edward Gerjuoy, "Science and Technology Resources for the Courts" (1989), published with revisions 14 Just. Sys. J. 358 (1991).

Bernard D. Goldstein and Mary Sue Henifin, "Toxicology and Protocol" (1991).

Leon Gordis, "An Introduction to Epidemiology for the Legal Setting" (1991).

Denis Hauptly and Kay Knapp, "A Focal Point for Science in the Courts" (1991).

Denis Hauptly, "Alternative Forms of Dispute Resolution in Science Cases" (1992).

Deborah Hensler, "Science in the Court: Is There a Role for Alternative Dispute Resolution?" (1989).

Sheila Jasanoff and Bert Black, "What Science Is and What It Is Not," in AAAS-ABA National Conference of Lawyers and Scientists Task Force on Science and Technology in the Courts (1991).

John Monahan and Laurens Walker, "Paper and Protocol for the Judicial Evaluation of Social Science Evidence" (1991).

Richard L. Revesz, "Specialized Courts and the Administrative Lawmaking System" (1989).

Maurice Rosenberg, "Preliminary Analysis of Issues of Science and Technology Facing the Federal Courts" (1989).

William K. Slate, II, "Strategic and Long-Range Planning in the Judiciary: Issues of Science and Technology" (1992).

Miron L. Straf, Stephen E. Fienberg, and Samuel Krislov, "Understanding and Evaluating Statistical Evidence in Litigation and Protocol" (1991).

Working Group of the Carnegie Commission on Science, Technology, and Government, "Suggested Agenda for Improvement" (1989), reprinted in Federal Courts Study Committee Working Papers and Subcommittee Reports, Vol. I (July 1, 1990).

APPENDIX B
BIOGRAPHIES OF MEMBERS OF THE TASK FORCE

Helene L. Kaplan, Of Counsel, Skadden, Arps, Slate, Meagher & Flom, serves as counsel or trustee of many science, arts, charitable, and educational institutions. She chairs the Board of Trustees of Barnard College and is treasurer of the Association of the Bar of the City of New York. Former chairman of the Board of Trustees of Carnegie Corporation of New York, Mrs. Kaplan currently serves as a trustee of that foundation, as well as trustee of the American Museum of Natural History; Committee on Economic Development; Commonwealth Fund; J. Paul Getty Trust; John Simon Guggenheim Memorial Foundation; Institute for Advanced Study; and Mount Sinai Hospital, Medical School and Medical Center. From 1985 to 1987, she was a member of the U.S. Secretary of State's Advisory Committee on South Africa; and from 1986 to 1990, she served as a member of New York Governor Cuomo's Task Force on Life and the Law, concerned with the legal and ethical implications of advances in medical technology. Mrs. Kaplan is a director of Chemical Banking Corporation and Chemical Bank, The May Department Stores Company, Metropolitan Life Insurance Company, Mobil Corporation, and NYNEX Corporation. She is a member of the American Academy of Arts and Sciences, the American Philosophical Society, and the Council on Foreign Relations. She is a graduate of Barnard College and New York University Law School, and is the recipient of an honorary doctorate of laws from Columbia University.

Alvin L. Alm is Director and Senior Vice President of Science Applications International Corporation. Mr. Alm was previously President and CEO of Alliance Technologies Corporation and Chairman of the Board and CEO of Thermo Analytical Corporation. At Harvard University, he was Director of the Harvard Energy Security Program. Mr. Alm served within the United States Government as Deputy Administrator and Assistant Administrator of Planning and Management of the Environmental Protection Agency, Assistant Secretary for Policy and Evaluation of the Department of Energy, Staff Director of the Council on Environmental Quality and the Bureau of the Budget. Mr. Alm is Chairman of the Research Strategies Advisory Council for the EPA Science Advisory Board and Chairman of the Subcommittee on Risk Strategies of the Relative Risk Reduction Strategies Committee of the Science Advisory Board. He is a member of the Board of Directors of the Environmental Law Institute and the Center for Hazardous Materials Research. He is a graduate of the University of Denver and the Maxwell Graduate School of Syracuse University.

Richard E. Ayres is a Partner in the Washington, DC, office of the law firm of O'Melveny & Myers. Mr. Ayres was co-founder of the Natural Resources Defense Council in 1970. From 1975 to 1991, he also served as Chairman of the National Clean Air Coalition, where he played a principal role in negotiating the new Clean Air Amendments of 1990 with representatives of EPA, the White House, Congress, and industry. He served as a presidential appointee on the National Commission on Air Quality from 1979 to 1981. Mr. Ayres has had broad experience in administrative proceedings, litigation, and legislative matters. He has participated in many of the major clean air rulemaking proceedings before the U.S. Environmental Protection Agency over the past two decades. These included proceedings regarding several federal air quality (health) standards, technology standards for new electric power plants, use of tall smokestacks to disperse pollution, and pollution rights trading. Mr. Ayres successfully negotiated the largest air pollution control settlement in the nation's history, settling a multicourt federal suit involving an investment of more than $1 billion in pollution control equipment and clean fuels. He has also handled a number of cases involving interpretation of the Clean Air Act before the federal Courts of Appeal, as well as the Supreme Court of the United States. In 1981 Mr. Ayres was honored by the Yale Law Association of Washington for his outstanding service to the public interest. His practice emphasizes environmental and related energy regulatory matters.

Sheila L. Birnbaum heads the products liability department of Skadden, Arps, Slate, Meagher & Flom. Ms. Birnbaum had previously been Counsel to the firm while she was Professor of Law and Associate Dean at New York University Law School. She was Professor of Law at Fordham University School of Law and has lectured extensively across the country. She is a Council Member of the American Law Institute and the ABA's Section of Torts and Insurance Practice, and a Member of the Second Circuit Committee on the Improvement of Civil Litigation. She took her law degree at New York University, and took undergraduate and graduate degrees from Hunter College.

Stephen G. Breyer is Chief Judge of the First Judicial Circuit of the United States (Maine, Massachusetts, New Hampshire, Rhode Island and Puerto Rico). Chief Judge Breyer is a member of the Judicial Conference of the United States and has served as a member of the U.S. Sentencing Commission. He previously served as Professor at Harvard Law School and Kennedy School of Government, Chief Counsel to the U.S. Senate Judiciary Committee and Special Counsel to its Subcommittee on Administrative Practices, Assistant Special Prosecutor for the Watergate Special Prosecution Force, and Special Assistant to the Assistant Attorney

General of the U.S. Department of Justice, and as a law clerk for the U.S. Supreme Court. Chief Judge Breyer is a member of the American Academy of Arts and Sciences and the American Law Institute. He has written books and articles in the field of administrative law and government regulation. A graduate of Stanford University and Oxford University, he graduated *magna cum laude* from Harvard Law School.

Harry L. Carrico is Chief Justice of the Supreme Court of Virginia following service as circuit judge and as trial justice. Chief Justice Carrico created the Commission on the Future of Virginia's Judicial System. He was previously in the private practice of law and served in the U.S. Navy. Co-Chairman of the National Judicial Council of State and Federal Courts, he is a member of the Committee on Federal–State Jurisdiction of the Judicial Conference of the United States. Chief Justice Carrico has served as President of the Conference of Chief Justices and as Chairman of the National Center for State Courts. He took his law degree from George Washington University Law School.

Theodore Cooper is Chairman of the Board and Chief Executive Officer of The Upjohn Company. Dr. Cooper previously held the positions of Vice Chairman of the Board and Executive Vice President. A former Dean of the Cornell University Medical College, he was Assistant Secretary for Health of the Department of Health, Education and Welfare. Dr. Cooper is a Director of the Upjohn Company; Metropolitan Life Insurance Company; Harris Bankcorp and Harris Trust and Savings Bank; Borden, Inc.; and Kellogg Company. He is a Trustee of St. Louis University and the University of Chicago. He has received numerous awards and honors, including the Gold Heart Award and the Department of Defense Distinguished Public Service Award.

Douglas Costle is a former administrator of the U.S. Environmental Protection Agency and former dean of Vermont Law School. Mr. Costle has also been a trial attorney in the Civil Rights Division of the U.S. Department of Justice and has served as an attorney for the U.S. Department of Commerce, Economic Development Administration. He worked as an associate with two San Francisco law firms before becoming senior staff associate to the President's Advisory Council on Executive Organization, in Washington, DC, where he played a key role in establishing the U.S. Environmental Protection Agency. Mr. Costle has served as commissioner to the Connecticut Department of Environmental Protection, as assistant director of the U.S. Congressional Budget Office, and as a fellow of the Smithsonian Institution's Woodrow Wilson International Center for Scholars. Mr. Costle has also been a visiting scholar at the Harvard School of Public Health and an adjunct lecturer in the John F. Kennedy School of Government. He is a graduate of Harvard University and the University of Chicago Law School.

E. Donald Elliott is a tenured professor of Law at Yale Law School, where he has taught since 1981. He also serves as a consultant to the law firm of Fried, Frank, Harris, Shriver & Jacobson, in New York and Washington. He has wide experience in the fields of environmental law, administrative law, and toxic torts. From July 1989 to August 1991, he served as Assistant Administrator and General Counsel of the Environmental Protection Agency. In that position, he served as chief legal advisor to EPA administrator William Reilly and headed a staff of over 125 lawyers with a docket of 450 cases. Before joining EPA, Professor Elliott served for five years as Special Litigation Counsel, Corporate Environmental Programs, General Electric Co., where he was responsible for the defense of GE's toxic tort cases. Professor Elliott is the author of over 30 articles and has lectured widely both here and abroad.

In July 1990, Professor Elliott was named as one of the top lawyers in the country in the fields of environmental law and toxic torts by the *National Law Journal*. He is a graduate of Yale College (Phi Beta Kappa, *summa cum laude*) and Yale Law School. Before joining the Yale Law School in 1981, Mr. Elliott was in private practice with a law firm in Washington, DC (Leva, Hawes, Symington, Martin & Oppenheimer) and served as a law clerk to US District Judge Gerhard Gesell and US Circuit Judge David Bazelon. Elliott has been a consultant to the Carnegie Commission on Science, Technology, and Government; the Federal Courts Study Committee; and the Administrative Conference of the United States, and has been Vice-Chair of the ABA Administrative Law Section's Committee on Separation of Powers.

Kenneth R. Feinberg is in the private practice of law in Washington, DC. Mr. Feinberg has served as Administrative Assistant to Senator Edward M. Kennedy and Special Counsel to the United States Senate Committee on the Judiciary. A former Assistant U.S. Attorney for the Southern District of New York, he has served as Adjunct Professor of Law at Georgetown University Law Center, the Graduate School of Political Management, and as Law Clerk to Chief Judge Stanley H. Fuld, New York State Court of Appeals. Mr. Feinberg was appointed Special Settlement Master, *In re: Agent Orange Product Liability Litigation*; Special Settlement Master, *In re: Eagle-Picher Industries, Inc.* (national asbestos personal injury/wrongful death class action); Special Settlement Master, *In re: Joint Eastern and Southern District Asbestos Litigation* (federal and state asbestos personal injury/wrongful death litigation arising out of exposures at the Brooklyn Navy Yard); Special Settlement Master, *County of Suffolk, et al. v. Long Island Lighting Co., et al.* (Shoreham Nuclear Facility class action); Special Settlement Master, *In re: Asbestos Personal Injury Litigation* (asbestos personal injury/wrongful death litigation pending in the Maryland State courts); Special Settlement Master, *In re: DES Cases* (federal and state personal injury/wrongful death DES litigation); Trustee, Dalkon Shield Claimants' Trust; and Member, Presidential Commission on Catastrophic Nuclear Accidents. He is Arbitrator, American Arbitration Association; Member, National Panel, Center for Public Resources; and Vice-Chair, Committee on Alternative Dispute Resolution, American Bar Association. He graduated *cum laude*, from the University of Massachusetts. Mr. Feinberg took his law degree from New York University School of Law, where he served as Articles Editor of the *Law Review*.

Robert W. Kastenmeier is Chairman of the National Commission on Judicial Discipline and Removal and a Distinguished Fellow of the Governance Institute. A Member of Congress for 32 years, he served as chairman of the subcommittee on courts for over 20 years. Mr. Kastenmeier was appointed by Chief Justice Rehnquist to serve as a member of the Federal Courts Study Committee. He was in the private practice of law and served as justice of the peace in Watertown, Wisconsin. Following service in the U.S. Army and the War Department, he took his law degree from the University of Wisconsin.

Donald Kennedy is President emeritus and Bing Professor of Environmental Studies at Stanford University, where he has held a variety of academic positions—Chairman of the Department of Biological Sciences, Chairman of the Program in Human Biology, Vice President and Provost, and President (1980–1992). Dr. Kennedy was appointed to the Benjamin Scott Crocker Professorship in Human Biology and received the Dinkelspiel Award, the University's highest honor for service to undergraduate education. Dr. Kennedy is a member of the National Academy of Sciences, the Institute of Medicine, and the American Philosophical Society; his research interests centered on nervous systems and the control of behavior. He has served on National Academy of Sciences committees on pesticide use and on improving the world's food supply, and is a director of the Health Effects Institute, Clean Sites, Inc., the California Nature Conservancy, and the California Commission on Campaign Financing. He was Senior Consultant to the Office of Science and Technology Policy in the Ford White House, and he served as Commissioner of the Food and Drug Administration during the Carter presidency. Dr. Kennedy was educated at Harvard University, from which he holds three degrees in biology.

Francis E. McGovern is Francis H. Hare Professor of Torts at the University of Alabama School of Law. Professor McGovern was previously Visiting Professor at Massachusetts Institute of Technology, Senior Associate at Harvard, and in the private practice of law. He is Advisor to the Board of Editors for the Manual for Complex Litigation, and a member of the American Bar Association Commission on Mass Torts and the American Law Institute. He is a graduate of Yale University and the University of Virginia School of Law.

Richard A. Merrill is Daniel Caplin Professor of Law at the University of Virginia School of Law and Special Counsel with the firm of Covington & Burling. Professor Merrill was previously in private practice and also served as General Counsel, U.S. Food and Drug Administration. He is a member of the American Law Institute and the Institute of Medicine. He served on the EPA's Biotechnology Science Advisory Committee, and on two Institute of Medicine Committees, looking at nutrition labeling and at FDA's use of advisory committees in product approval. A Rhodes Scholar, he took his undergraduate and law degrees from Columbia University and a masters degree from Oxford University.

Richard A. Meserve is a partner with the Washington, DC, law firm of Covington & Burling. His practice focuses on legal issues that involve substantial technical content, including environmental and toxic tort litigation, nuclear licensing, and the counseling of scientific societies and high-technology companies. He has served on a variety of committees of the National Academies of Sciences and Engineering. He served as Chairman of the Committee to Provide Interim Oversight of the DOE Nuclear Weapons Complex and of the Committee to Assess Technical and Safety Issues at DOE Reactors. He previously served as a member of two committees that examined controls on high-technology exports. Dr. Meserve is now serving as Co-chairman of the National Conference of Lawyers and Scientists, a group sponsored by the American Bar Association and the American Association for the Advancement of Science. He is a Fellow of the American Physical Society and serves on the Society's Panel on Public Affairs. He is a member of the Advisory Council of the Princeton Plasma Physics Laboratory; of the Advisory Board of the MIT Center for Technology, Policy, and Industrial Development; and of the Board of Overseers for the Natural Sciences for Tufts University. He served for four years as legal counsel to the President's Science and Technology Advisor, where he worked on policies relating to the health of science, industrial innovation, and energy. He was also formerly a clerk to Justice Harry A. Blackmun, United States Supreme Court, and to Judge Benjamin Kaplan, Massachusetts Supreme Judicial Court. Dr. Meserve received a B.A. from Tufts University, a Ph.D. in Applied Physics from Stanford University, and a J.D. from Harvard Law School.

Gilbert S. Omenn is Professor of Medicine and of Environmental Health and Dean of the School of Public Health and Community Medicine at the University of Washington, Seattle. He is Principal Investigator of the Carotene and Retinol Efficacy Trial (CARET) to prevent lung cancer and Director of the Center for Health Promotion in Older Adults. Dr. Omenn served as a deputy to Frank Press, President Carter's Science and Technology Advisor and

Director of the White House Office of Science and Technology Policy, and then as an Associate Director of the Office of Management and Budget. He served on the National Cancer Advisory Board and the National Heart, Lung and Blood Advisory Council. He was a Visiting Senior Fellow at the Woodrow Wilson School of Public and International Affairs, Princeton University, and then the first Science & Public Policy Fellow at The Brookings Institution, Washington, DC. With economist Lester Lave, he published *Clearing the Air: Reforming the Clean Air Act* (1981). He served on the National Commission on the Environment and now serves on the National Risk Assessment and Risk Management Commission mandated by the 1990 Clean Air Act. He is a member of the Institute of Medicine and served on its Council. He has chaired the Board on Environmental Studies and Toxicology of the National Research Council, and the EPRI EMF Health Effects Technical Advisory Board. He serves on the Board of Directors of Rohm & Haas Company, Amgen, and Immune Response Corporation. He earned his B.A. from Princeton, M.D. from Harvard, and Ph.D. in Genetics from the University of Washington. He was a White House Fellow at the Atomic Energy Commission.

Joseph G. Perpich is Vice President for Grants and Special Programs of the Howard Hughes Medical Institute. Dr. Perpich served as the Associate Director for Planning and Evaluation at the National Institutes of Health and later as Vice President for Planning and Business Development at several biotechnology companies in the Washington area. He joined the Howard Hughes Medical Institute to develop a grants program in science education, which now ranges from grade school activities to postgraduate research training. Dr. Perpich is a graduate of the University of Minnesota Medical School and completed his residency in psychiatry at the Massachusetts General Hospital and the National Institute of Mental Health. He is also a graduate of the Georgetown University Law Center. Dr. Perpich is a fellow of the American Psychiatric Association and a member of the Bar of the District of Columbia. He is a member of the Board of Advisors of the American Board of Internal Medicine. Dr. Perpich has broad experience in science and technology policy—as a congressional fellow with the U.S. Senate Committee on Labor and Public Welfare, Subcommittee on Health, as chairman of the Biotechnology Advisory Committee of the Pharmaceutical Manufacturers Association, as a member of national, state, and local science and technology committees, and on the editorial boards of journals addressing law, science, and society. Dr. Perpich is the author or editor of several articles and books on federal R&D/regulatory policy and the biotechnology industry, including *Biotechnology in Society: Private Initiatives and Public Oversight* (Pergamon Press 1986).

Paul D. Rheingold is with Rheingold & McGowen, P.C. A trial lawyer, Mr. Rheingold represents plaintiffs in mass litigation and product liability. He was previously Lecturer on Law at Harvard Law School and Rutgers Law School, and Adjunct Professor at Fordham Law School. Overseer for the Institute for Civil Justice of Rand Institute, he is Advisor for the American Law Institute Restatement on Products Liability. Mr. Rheingold chairs the Planning Commission for the City of Rye, New York. He is a member of the American Bar Association's Commission on Mass Torts, and previously chaired the Manufacturers' Liability Committee and Special Committee on Punitive Damages of the ABA's Litigation Section. Mr. Rheingold chaired the New York State Bar Association's Committee on Tort Reparations, and was a member of the Advisory Committee on Product Liability for the U.S. Department of Commerce. He is a graduate of Oberlin College and Harvard Law School (*cum laude*).

Maurice Rosenberg is Harold R. Medina Professor of Procedural Jurisprudence Emeritus, Columbia University School of Law. Professor Rosenberg has served as Special Assistant to the Attorney General, and as Assistant Attorney General with the U.S. Department of Justice. He was in the private practice of law following service as Law Clerk to Judge Stanley H. Fuld, New York Court of Appeals. In World War II, he served in the infantry and military government. He has written *The Pretrial Conference and Effective Justice*, 1964; *Conflict of Laws* (with Reese and Hay), 1990; *Civil Procedure* (with Smit and Dreyfuss), 1990; *Justice on Appeal* (with Carrington and Meador), 1976; *Appellate Justice in New York* (with Hopkins and MacCrate), 1983. Professor Rosenberg is a member of the American Academy of Arts and Sciences. He was chairman of the Advisory Council for Appellate Justice, 1971–1976; chairman of the Council on the Role of Courts, 1978–1979; and president of AALS, 1973; and he has been a trustee of the Practicing Law Institute since 1975. Professor Rosenberg is currently serving as academic consultant to the Appellate Judges Seminar Series and as chairman of the ABA Standing Committee on Federal Judicial Improvements. He is a graduate of Syracuse University and Columbia University School of Law, where he was Editor-in-Chief of the *Columbia Law Review*.

Oscar M. Ruebhausen, retired presiding partner of Debevoise & Plimpton, practiced law for nearly 50 years. During those years he engaged in numerous science-related activities. He was General Counsel to the Office of Scientific Research and Development in Washington, DC, from 1944 to 1946. Subsequently, he has chaired, or been a member of, a wide range of commissions, task forces, panels, and committees focused on science/social policy issues. These have been public (at both the federal and state level) and private (supported by foundations or bar associations) in sponsorship. He has also been chairman, or a director, of a number of business corporations and not-for-profit organizations, has written for professional journals, and is a past president of The Association of the Bar of the City of New York. He is a graduate of Dartmouth College (*summa cum laude*) and Yale Law School (*cum laude*), where he was Note Editor of the *Yale Law Journal*.

Pamela Ann Rymer was appointed United States Circuit Judge for the Court of Appeals for the Ninth Circuit (Alaska, Arizona, California, Guam, Hawaii, Idaho, Montana, Nevada, N. Mariana Islands, Oregon, & Washington) following service as United States District Judge for the Central District of California. Judge Rymer was previously in the private practice of law. Judge Rymer is a trustee of Stanford University and was chair of the California Post-secondary Education Commission. She is on the Board of Directors of the Constitutional Rights Foundation and is a member of the Judicial Conference of the United States Committee on Criminal Law and Probation, and the Education Commission of the States, Task Force on State Policy and Independent Higher Education. She is a member of the American Bar Association Civil Justice Reform Coordinating Committee, the State Bar of California Antitrust and Trade Regulation Committee, and the Los Angeles County Bar Association Committee on Professionalism. A graduate of Vassar College, Judge Rymer took her law degree at Stanford University Law School.

Irving S. Shapiro joined the law firm of Skadden, Arps, Slate, Meagher & Flom following his retirement as Chairman of the Board and Chief Executive Officer of the DuPont Company. Mr. Shapiro came to DuPont as an attorney in the Legal Department after serving in the U.S. Department of Justice during the Roosevelt and Truman Administrations, where he specialized in practice before the Supreme Court. His work in the Legal Department emphasized antitrust litigation and providing counsel to various manufacturing departments on a wide range of business problems. During the eight years Mr. Shapiro spent with the Justice Department, from 1943 to 1951, he specialized in practice before the Supreme Court and the various Circuit Courts of Appeal. He worked for eighteen months at the Office of

Price Administration in Washington, helping to establish a rationing program at the inception of World War II. He played a major role in the antitrust case of the 1950s and early 1960s that forced DuPont to divest itself of General Motors stock. In 1965 he was appointed assistant general counsel of the company. Mr. Shapiro is a former trustee of the Conference Board and the Ford Foundation. He served for two years as chairman of the Business Roundtable and served two years as vice chairman of the Business Council. He is chairman of the Trustees of the Howard Hughes Medical Institute, and is a member of the American Academy of Arts and Sciences and the American Philosophical Society. He is a Director of AEA Investors Inc. and Morgan Trust Company of Florida. He is a Senior Counselor on the Board of Counselors of Bechtel Group, Inc. He is a Member of the Advisory Council of Wells Fargo & Company. He is a graduate of the University of Minnesota and its law school.

William K. Slate, II, is president of the Justice Research Institute, which is located in Philadelphia and Washington, DC. He previously served as director of the congressionally mandated Federal Courts Study Committee, CEO of the Virginia State Bar, Circuit Executive for the Third Judicial Circuit of the United States, and Clerk of the United States Court of Appeals for the Fourth Circuit; he also served with the United States Department of Justice. He has practiced law, been an adjunct professor of law, judicial administration and management, and was a visiting professor at Seton Hall Law School in Newark, New Jersey. He is the Reporter to the District Court of the Virgin Islands for the Civil Justice Reform Act of 1990. Mr. Slate is an elected member of the American Law Institute and is a member of the ABA Standing Committee on Federal Judicial Improvements. He is a founder of the Council for Court Excellence in Washington DC. Mr. Slate was a member of the Virginia Commission on the Future of the Judiciary Task Force on Technology. A graduate of Wake Forest University and the University of Richmond School of Law, he holds an M.B.A. from the Wharton School of the University of Pennsylvania. He is a graduate Fellow of the Institute for Court Management and an S.M.G. graduate of the John F. Kennedy School of Government at Harvard University. He has also engaged in graduate studies in comparative law at Oxford University.

Patricia M. Wald is United States Circuit Judge for the District of Columbia Circuit. Judge Wald previously served as Chief Judge of the circuit, Assistant Attorney General for Legislative Affairs with the U.S. Department of Justice and Staff Attorney of its Office of Criminal Justice, Litigation Director with the Mental Health Law Project, director of the Office of Policy and Issues with the Sergeant Shriver vice presidential campaign, and co-director of the Ford Foundation Drug Abuse Research Project. She also served as an attorney with the Center for Law and Public Policy, the National Commission on the Causes and Prevention of Violence, and the Neighborhood Advisory Committee on Civil Disorder. Judge Wald was a Member of the National Conference on Bail and Criminal Justice and a Consultant for the President's Commission on Law Enforcement and Administration of Criminal Justice. She has been a member of the Committee on Codes of Conduct of the Judicial Conference of the United States and is a member of the Executive Committee of the American Law Institute and its Second Vice President. She is a Fellow with the American Bar Association, a member of the American Academy of Arts and Sciences, and has served with the National Science Foundation–National Research Council Committee on Law Enforcement and Administration of Justice. She is a graduate of Connecticut College for Women (Phi Beta Kappa, Winthrop Scholar) and Yale Law School (Order of Coif).

Jack B. Weinstein is United States District Judge for the Eastern District of New York. He was Chief Judge from April 30, 1980, to March 31, 1988. Judge Weinstein is a member of the American Law Institute and the American Academy of Arts and Sciences. He has served as a member of the Subcommittee on Federal Jurisdiction of the Committee on Court Administration of the Judicial Conference of the United States; the Advisory Committee on Rules of Evidence; the Special Advisory Group to the Chief Justice on Problems Relating to Federal Civil Litigation; and the Ad Hoc Advisory Committee on the Administrative Office. He was a member of the Judicial Conference of the United States, 1983–1986. Judge Weinstein was Special Counsel to the New York Joint Legislative Committee on Motor Vehicle Problems; Reporter and Consultant on Practice and Procedure to the New York State Temporary Commission on the Courts; member of the Advisory Committee on Practice and Procedure of the New York State Senate Finance Committee; member of the City of New York Advisory Narcotics Council; and County Attorney of Nassau County, New York. He served as Lieutenant in the United States Navy during World War II. He is a graduate of Brooklyn College and Columbia Law School, where he now teaches part-time.

Senior Consultant

Margaret A. Berger is Associate Dean and Professor of Law at Brooklyn Law School. After graduating from Radcliffe College and Columbia Law School and spending some time in the private practice of law, she served as a law clerk to Judge Jack B. Weinstein of the District Court for the Eastern District of New York. At Brooklyn Law School, she specializes in Evidence and Civil Procedure. She is the co-author of Weinstein's *Evidence* and Weinstein's *Evidence Manual*, and is also a co-author of a casebook on evidence (with Weinstein, Mansfield and Abrams). She currently serves by appointment of the Chief Justice of the United States as Reporter for the Judicial Conference of the United States' Advisory Committee on the Federal Rules of Evidence. She has been a visiting professor of law at New York University and Harvard University. She is a member of the American Law Institute, and has served on numerous committees of the American Bar Association, the Association of the Bar of the City of New York, the Second Circuit and the Eastern District of New York. She is currently serving as a consultant to the advisory group in the Eastern District of New York that is drafting an implementation plan on the Civil Justice Reform Act of 1990.

Staff

Steven G. Gallagher is a Senior Staff Associate with the Commission. Mr. Gallagher previously served as Counsel to the Federal Courts Study Committee, as Assistant Circuit Executive for the Third Judicial Circuit, and as Staff Attorney for the United States Court of Appeals for the Third Circuit. He administered two national conferences of the Federal Judges Association and served five years with the United States Air Force. A graduate of the College of Engineering and Technology of the Southern Illinois University and of Rutgers University School of Law–Camden, he is completing his graduate work at the University of Pennsylvania.

David Z. Beckler is Associate Director for the Carnegie Commission on Science, Technology, and Government. He was the Senior Assistant to the President's Science Advisor and Executive Officer of the President's Science Advisory Committee from 1956 to 1972. From 1976 to 1983, Mr. Beckler was Director for Science, Technology and Industry of the Organization for Economic Cooperation and Development in Paris, France. He is a graduate of the University of Rochester (chemical engineering) and the George Washington University Law School.

Consultant

Elizabeth H. Esty is a lawyer, adjunct professor, and consultant. Ms. Esty clerked for the Honorable Robert E. Keeton before joining the law firm of Sidley & Austin in Washington, DC. While at Sidley & Austin, she helped formulate organized medicine's proposal for comprehensive medical malpractice reform. She has participated in the Institute of Medicine's examination of Medical Professional Liability and the Delivery of Obstetrical Care, and in the Georgetown University Program for Science and Law's conference on Planning Scientific Evidence. She has been an adjunct professor at American University and a guest lecturer at Stanford University's Washington program. She received her A.B. from Harvard University, was a Rotary Graduate Fellow at the Institut d'Etudes Politiques de Paris, and graduated from Yale Law School.

APPENDIX C
APPRECIATION

In view of the interdisciplinary nature of both the Task Force and of the issues to be addressed, the Task Force's activities included initiatives with institutions and individuals in both the judicial and scientific communities. The Task Force is indebted to the following people who have contributed to its efforts:

Fred R. Anderson	Leon Gordis
Linda Bailey	Denis Hauptly
Troyen A. Brennan	Mary Sue Henifin
Edward Burger, Jr.	Deborah R. Hensler
José A. Cabranes	Sally T. Hillsman
Joe S. Cecil	Sheila Jasanoff
Warren I. Cikins	Michael E. Kunz
Rochelle Cooper Dreyfuss	Kay Knapp
Stephen E. Fienberg	Samuel Krislov
Edward Gerjuoy	Kevin McCarthy
Bernard D. Goldstein	Daniel J. Meador

Arthur Miller
John Monahan
Richard L. Revesz
Thomas D. Rowe, Jr.
Michael J. Saks
Austin Sarat
Linda Silverman

Dale Sipes
Miron L. Straf
David I. Tevelin
Carl W. Tobias
Laurens Walker
Joseph F. Weis

1. David M. O'Brien, *What Process Is Due? Courts and Science-Policy Disputes*, 2 (Russell Sage Foundation: New York, 1987).

2. One study of 2,000 federal district court cases over a 3-year period found 49 to involve significant technology or science problems. *Science, Technology and Judicial Decision-Making: An Exploratory Discussion* 15 (ed. J.D. Nyhart, 1977).

3. A consultant's report submitted to the Federal Courts Study Committee in 1989 estimated that scientific and technical issues arose in 20–30 percent of court cases. A recent survey by the Federal Judicial Center found that approximately 8 percent of federal cases in which expert testimony was offered involved scientific specialties, with another 39.8 percent involving medical or mental health experts. Joe S. Cecil and Molly Treadway Johnson, *Expertise of Witnesses Offering Testimony in 326 Recent Federal Civil Trials*, Federal Judicial Center (March 1992 unpublished manuscript).

4. Samuel R. Gross, *Expert Evidence*, 1991 Wisc. L. Rev. 1113, 1119. Of the experts who testified, half were medical doctors, and another 9 percent were other medical professionals; engineers, scientists and related experts made up the next

largest category (nearly 20 percent). In short, nearly two-thirds of the California cases that went to verdict involved significant scientific or technical issues. A majority of the 529 California trials studied involved wrongful death or personal injuries, with medical malpractice and product liability cases also accounting for an unusually high proportion of expert testimony.

5. Remarks of Judge Harold E. Leventhal, reported in *Science, Technology and Judicial Decision-making: An Exploratory Discussion*, note 2 above.

6. Year-end address of Chief Justice Rehnquist, reprinted in *The Third Branch*, p. 4 (January 1992).

7. *New York Times*, June 8, 1992, p. D1, col. 3.

8. Learned Hand, *Historical and Practical Considerations Regarding Expert Testimony*, 15 Harv. L. Rev. 40, 56 (1901).

9. Joe S. Cecil and Thomas E. Willging, *Defining a Role for Court-Appointed Experts*, 4 FJC Directions 6 (1992).

10. Sheila Jasanoff, *What Judges Should Know About the Sociology of Science*, 32 Jurimetrics J. 345, 349 (1992).

11. Harold E. Leventhal, *Environmental Decisionmaking and the Role of the Courts*, 122 U. Pa. L. Rev. 509 (1974).

12. Federal Courts Study Act, Pub. L. No. 100–702, 102 Stat. 4644 (1988).

13. Report of the Federal Courts Study Committee (April 2, 1990).

14. Memorandum of Action, Executive Committee of the Judicial Conference of the United States 5 (May 18, 1990).

15. Margaret A. Berger, *Procedural and Evidentiary Mechanisms for Dealing with Experts in Toxic Tort Litigation: A Critique and Proposal* (Carnegie Commission: October 1991).

16. For all the outcry over inconsistent results in the many cases alleging that Bendectin caused birth defects, at this writing there is apparently only one federal Bendectin case in which a plaintiff ultimately won, and that plaintiff has apparently not yet collected a judgment. *See* Joseph Sanders, *The Bendectin Litigation: A Case Study in the Life Cycle of Mass Torts*, 43 Hast. L.J. 301 (1992). It should be noted, however, that the Supreme Court granted certiorari on October 13, 1992, in a Bendectin case in which the Ninth Circuit had affirmed a grant of summary judgment to the defendant. *Daubert v. Merrell Dow Pharmaceuticals, Inc.*, 951 F.2d 1128 (9th Cir. 1991), *cert. granted*, 61 U.S.L.W. 3284 (1992).

17. Some of these issues may be resolved by the Supreme Court's grant of certiorari in *Daubert v. Merrell Dow Pharmaceuticals, Inc.*, 951 F.2d 1128 (9th Cir. 1991), *cert. granted*, 61 U.S.L.W. 3284 (1992). The Carnegie Commission filed a brief *amicus curiae* in support of neither party before the Supreme Court suggesting an evidentiary and procedural approach to the admissibility of expert testimony based on science.

18. Catherine Pierce, *Survey of Judicial Education Involving Science and Technology* (1992, Carnegie Commission, unpublished manuscript).

19. Several recent developments reflect the interest in this area: the Judicial Conference of the United States has created a committee on long-range planning, the Administrative Office of the U.S. Courts has created a long-range planning di-

vision, and the National State–Federal Judicial Council is considering establishing a similar entity.

20. AAAS–ABA National Conference of Lawyers and Scientists Task Force on Science and Technology in the Courts, *Enhancing the Availability of Reliable and Impartial Scientific and Technical Expertise to the Federal Courts* (1991, Carnegie Commission, unpublished manuscript).

21. The Center for Law, Science, and Technology has conducted a survey of the substantial and growing number of academic law and science programs that currently exist around the country. L. Crowley, D. Illman, and D. VanBeck, *Survey of Law, Science, and Technology Studies in U.S. Law Schools* (April 28, 1992; University of Washington School of Law, Center for Law, Science, and Technology). Dissemination of this survey would alert judicial educators and academics to others who share their interests.

GLOSSARY

Adversarial process — requires that lawyers must zealously make the most effective statement possible of their client's case. This process ensures that the evidence and the issues will be fully explored and presented so that the impartial fact-finder will be enabled to reach an informed and just decision.

Alternative dispute resolution (ADR) — the term applied to a variety of mechanisms for resolving disputes outside of the traditional legal system. Such mechanisms include binding or nonbinding arbitration, adjudication by specialized nonjudicial tribunals, and fault or no-fault administrative proceedings.

American Judicature Society (AJS) — an independent national, membership-based organization of more than 20,000 judges, attorneys and other citizens dedicated to improving the administration of justice.

American Law Institute (ALI) — a private nonprofit organization established to promote the clarification and simplification of the law and its better adaptation to social needs, to secure the better administration of justice, and to encourage and carry on scholarly and scientific legal work. ALI is member-supported, but it also receives foundation grants. Members are elected by its council with total membership limited to 2,500.

Amicus curiae — literally, friend of the court. Individuals or organizations who are not parties to a case but who have a strong interest in the subject matter of a case may file a brief stating their views and bringing the expertise of their constituencies to the attention of the court.

Certiorari — generally used in reference to the Supreme Court of the United States, the writ of certiorari is a discretionary device through which the Court can review cases that turn on questions of federal law. In recent years the Court has typically granted between 100 and 200 of the several thousand petitions for a writ of certiorari filed each year by losing parties that have completed (exhausted) all other state or federal appeals.

Consolidation of cases — a procedure under Federal Rule of Civil Procedure 42 or analogous state rules where actions involving a common question of law or fact pending before a court can be consolidated for joint hearing or trial on any or all matters as "may tend to avoid unnecessary costs or delay." See also *Federal rules*, *Mass tort*, and *Multidistrict litigation*.

Discovery — the pretrial devices that a party in a legal case can use to obtain facts and information from another party. Under the Federal Rules of Civil Procedure, discovery tools include depositions (sworn statements in response to written or oral questions), written interrogatories, production of documents, and physical examination.

Federal Courts Study Committee (FCSC) — created by Congress in 1988, the FCSC was established to examine the problems and issues currently facing the federal courts, to develop a long-range plan for the future of the federal judiciary, and to report its recommendations. The fifteen members of the Committee were appointed by the Chief Justice of the United States and were broadly representative of the interests affected by the federal courts.

Federal Judicial Center (FJC) — the research, education, and planning arm of the federal judicial system that was established by Congress in 1967 (28 U.S.C. §§ 620–629), on the recommendation of the Judicial Conference of the United States. The Chief Justice of the United States chairs the Center's Board, which also includes the director of the Administrative Office of the U.S. Courts and six judges elected by the Judicial Conference of the United States. The Board appoints a director to supervise the activities of the Center.

Federal Judicial Center Foundation — a private, nonprofit corporation established by Congress in 1988 and chartered by the District of Columbia to receive gifts made to support the work of the Center. The foundation is governed by a seven-person board, whose members are appointed by the Chief Justice of the United States, the President Pro Tempore of the Senate, and the Speaker of the House of Representatives.

Federal Rules — procedural rules adopted pursuant to a rulemaking authority that Congress has delegated to the judiciary while retaining the right to veto or modify the rules. The Federal Rules of Civil Procedure govern all civil actions and the Federal Rules of Criminal Procedure govern criminal actions. The Federal Rules of Evidence govern the admissability of evidence in both civil and criminal cases in federal courts. The corresponding rules of procedure and evidence in many state jurisdictions are modeled after the federal rules.

Institute for Civil Justice, the RAND Corporation — established within the RAND Corporation in 1979, ICJ performs independent, objective policy analysis and research on the American civil justice system. ICJ is supported by pooled grants from corporations, private foundations, trade and professional associations and individuals. RAND is a private, nonprofit institution, incorporated in 1948, which engages in nonpartisan research and analysis on problems of national security and the public welfare.

Judicial Conference of the United States — was created by Congress (28 U.S.C. § 331) in 1922, to "serve as the principal policymaking body concerned with the administration of the United States Courts." The Chief Justice of the United States is the presiding officer. Membership includes the Chief Judge of each judicial circuit, the Chief Judge of the Court of International Trade, and a district judge from each regional judicial circuit who is elected for a term of three years by the circuit and district judges of the circuit represented. The Conference operates through a network of committees. The Chief Justice has sole authority to make committee appointments.

Magistrate judges — are judicial officers appointed by United States District Courts for fixed terms of service. Authority is delegated by district court judges to magistrate judges for the conduct of certain judicial business such as pretrial hearings or consideration of motions by the parties. The extent of such delegated authority is limited by the Constitution and by legislation.

Mass tort — the term applied to a category of cases in which many plaintiffs allege a similar injury or injuries caused by an action or product of a single defendant or group of defendants. The claims related to Agent Orange, asbestos exposure and IUDs are examples.

Multidistrict litigation — when civil actions involving one or more common questions of fact are pending in several different federal district courts, federal law allows the cases to be coordinated and consolidated for pretrial procedures under a single judge. 28 U.S.C. § 1407. A Judicial Panel on Multidistrict Litigation assigns and transfers such cases which are governed by the "Manual for Complex Litigation" and the "Rules of Procedure of the Judicial Panel on Multidistrict Litigation."

National Center for State Courts (NCSC) — a private nonprofit organization founded in 1971 by the Conference of Chief Justices and the Conference of State Court Administrators to help state courts better serve litigants and the public. The NCSC provides an information exchange, research, education and training, and direct assistance to state courts. Its principal financial support comes from state governments, but it also receives federal and private grants.

National Childhood Vaccine Compensation Act — the newest and most structured legislatively created program for mass tort resolution. The issue of causation is eliminated by assuming causation if specified symptoms occur within a defined period of time after a child receives a specified vaccination. Special masters of the United States Claims Court award damages according to a compensation table. Awards are paid from a special pool of funds contributed by the vaccine manufacturers in lieu of defending expensive lawsuits. Even if the petitioner loses, the program pays costs and attorneys' fees. A victim may reject an award and proceed to suit in federal or state court, but only one person has done so in several hundred concluded cases.

Pretrial — a term applied to the filings and proceedings before the commencement of an actual trial. Common pretrial activities in S&T cases include discovery, pretrial conferences to narrow issues to be tried, pretrial hearings to clarify the scope of expert testimony and depositions.

Special masters — under Federal Rule of Civil Procedure 53 and analogous state rules, a judge can appoint a "master" to assist the court in a specific exceptional case. This person's powers and duties vary, depending on the judge and the case, and can include such matters as supervising discovery of evidence, taking of evidence, overseeing expert depositions, and meeting with the parties to clarify issues for trial.

State Justice Institute (SJI) — a private, nonprofit corporation established in 1984 by an Act of Congress (42 U.S.C. § 10701) for the purpose of providing financial support to projects designed to improve the administration of justice in the state courts. Its governing Board of Directors, consisting of 11 members appointed by the President with the advice and consent of the Senate, is statutorily composed of six judges, a state court administrator, and four members of the public, of whom no more than two may be of the same political party.

Summary judgment — a procedure under Federal Rule of Civil Procedure 56 and equivalent state rules where any party in a civil action can ask the court to rule in its favor on a claim. The party must show that there is no genuine issue of material fact (that there is no factual dispute that would alter the legal outcome) and that it is entitled to prevail as a matter of law. Summary judgment takes place *before* a trial and is a way of resolving issues without a trial.

Toxic tort—a term loosely applied to legal cases alleging injury or disease caused by exposure to hazardous substances and products. The term encompasses the claims alleging injuries such as lung disease and cancer from asbestos exposure, Bendectin and IUD injuries, and environmentally induced harm such as radiation-induced injury and disease caused by exposure to pesticides.

MEMBERS OF THE CARNEGIE COMMISSION ON SCIENCE, TECHNOLOGY, AND GOVERNMENT

William T. Golden (Co-Chair)
Chairman of the Board
American Museum of Natural History

Joshua Lederberg (Co-Chair)
University Professor
Rockefeller University

David Z. Robinson (Executive Director)
Carnegie Commission on Science,
     Technology, and Government

Richard C. Atkinson
Chancellor
University of California, San Diego

Norman R. Augustine
Chair & Chief Executive Officer
Martin Marietta Corporation

John Brademas
President Emeritus
New York University

Lewis M. Branscomb
Albert Pratt Public Service Professor
Science, Technology, and Public Policy
     Program
John F. Kennedy School of Government
Harvard University

Jimmy Carter
Former President of the United States

William T. Coleman, Jr.
Attorney
O'Melveny & Myers

Sidney D. Drell
Professor and Deputy Director
Stanford Linear Accelerator Center

Daniel J. Evans
Chairman
Daniel J. Evans Associates

General Andrew J. Goodpaster (Ret.)
Chairman
Atlantic Council of The United States

Shirley M. Hufstedler
Attorney
Hufstedler, Kaus & Ettinger

Admiral B. R. Inman (Ret.)

Helene L. Kaplan
Attorney
Skadden, Arps, Slate, Meagher & Flom

Donald Kennedy
Bing Professor of Environmental Science
Institute for International Studies, and
President Emeritus
Stanford University

Charles McC. Mathias, Jr.
Attorney
Jones, Day, Reavis & Pogue

William J. Perry*
Chairman & Chief Executive Officer
Technology Strategies & Alliances, Inc.

Robert M. Solow
Institute Professor
Department of Economics
Massachusetts Institute of Technology

H. Guyford Stever
Former Director
National Science Foundation

Sheila E. Widnall
Associate Provost and Abby Mauze
     Rockefeller Professor of Aeronautics
     and Astronautics
Massachusetts Institute of Technology

Jerome B. Wiesner
President Emeritus
Massachusetts Institute of Technology

---

* Through February 1993

Alice M. Rivlin[†]
Senior Fellow
Economics Department
Brookings Institution

Oscar M. Ruebhausen
Retired Presiding Partner
Debevoise & Plimpton

Jonas Salk
Founding Director
Salk Institute for Biological Studies

Maxine F. Singer
President
Carnegie Institution of Washington

Dick Thornburgh
Undersecretary General
Department of Administration and
   Management
United Nations

Admiral James D. Watkins (Ret.)[‡]
Former Chief of Naval Operations

Herbert F. York
Director Emeritus
Institute on Global Conflict and
   Cooperation
University of California, San Diego

Charles A. Zraket
Trustee
The MITRE Corporation

———————————

* Through April 1990
† Through January 1993
‡ Through January 1989

TASK FORCE ON SCIENCE AND TECHNOLOGY IN JUDICIAL AND REGULATORY DECISION MAKING

Helene L. Kaplan, Chair
Attorney
Skadden, Arps, Slate, Meagher & Flom

Alvin L. Alm
Director and Senior Vice President
Science Applications Int'l Corporation

Richard E. Ayres
Attorney
O'Melveny & Myers

Sheila L. Birnbaum
Attorney
Skadden, Arps, Slate, Meagher & Flom

Stephen G. Breyer
Chief Judge
United States Court of Appeals
   for the First Circuit

Harry L. Carrico
Chief Justice
Supreme Court of Virginia

Theodore Cooper
Chairman & Chief Executive Officer
The Upjohn Company

Douglas M. Costle
Former Administrator
U.S. Environmental Protection Agency

E. Donald Elliott
Professor of Law
Yale Law School

Kenneth R. Feinberg
Attorney
Kenneth R. Feinberg & Associates

Robert W. Kastenmeier
Chairman
National Commission on Judicial
   Discipline and Removal

Donald Kennedy
Bing Professor of Environmental Science
Institute for International Studies, and
President Emeritus
Stanford University